A Dog
Walks
into a
Nursing
Home

Sue Halpern

RIVERHEAD BOOKS

a member of Penguin Group (USA) Inc.

New York

2013

A Dog Walks into a Nursing Home

Lessons in the Good Life
from an
Unlikely Teacher

RIVERHEAD BOOKS
Published by the Penguin Group
Penguin Group (USA) Inc., 375 Hudson Street,
New York, New York 10014, USA

USA · Canada · UK · Ireland · Australia
New Zealand · India · South Africa · China

Penguin Books Ltd, Registered Offices: 80 Strand, London WC2R 0RL, England
For more information about the Penguin Group visit penguin.com

Library of Congress Cataloging-in-Publication Data

Halpern, Sue.
A dog walks into a nursing home : lessons in the good life from an
unlikely teacher / Sue Halpern.
p.   cm
ISBN 978-1-59448-720-0 (hardback)
1. Human-animal relationships.   2. Dogs—Therapeutic use.
3. Dogs—Training.   4. Halpern, Sue.   I. Title.
QL85.H35   2013   2013003605
636.7'0835—dc23

Printed in the United States of America
3   5   7   9   10   8   6   4   2

Book design by Gretchen Achilles

Some names and identifying characteristics have been changed
to protect the privacy of the individuals involved.

*Penguin is committed to publishing works of quality and integrity. In that spirit,
we are proud to offer this book to readers; however, the story,
the experiences, and the words are the author's alone.*

ALWAYS LEARNING   PEARSON

For Warren and Barry King

A Dog
Walks
into a
Nursing
Home

Introduction

Pransky, my soon-to-be ten-year-old dog, is lying on the living room couch, her body filling it end to end, for though she is not a big dog, she is double-jointed, which means that her hips lay out flat. If I weren't typing this I'd be stretched out next to her because I'm tired, too, as I often am on Tuesday afternoons. Every other day of the week, Pransky is a carefree country dog who operates by instinct, roaming the meadow around our house. But Tuesday mornings we spend time at the county nursing home, going door-to-door dispensing canine companionship and good cheer. Working at the nursing home requires us to pay attention—Pransky to me, to her surroundings, and to the people she is meeting, and me to her, to our surroundings, and to the people we are meeting. After three years you'd think we would have gotten tougher or more robust, but that's never happened and probably never will.

When I first considered training Pransky to be a therapy dog she was in her late adolescence. Dog years being what they are, she is now about the same age as most of the people in the nursing home. Even so, the words "work" and "walk" still get her to her feet in a unit of time that is less than a second. Is she better at her job, more empathetic, now that she, too, is of a certain age? I doubt it. I doubt it because I don't think she could be more empathetic.

As foreign as the nursing home environment was to both of us when we first started visiting County, it was a little less so to me, since my first job was at a medical school in a teaching hospital where I sometimes went on rounds. I was in my late twenties, with a newly minted doctorate, hired to teach ethics to second-year students. This should tell you all you need to know about how seriously that place took the ethical part of medical education: at that age I had about as much experience with the complicated ethical dilemmas of sick people and their families as the second-years in my class had treating sick people and dealing with those ethical dilemmas, which is to say, basically, none. Still, reality was not our mandate. We were supposed to consider what might happen "if," and then think through the best "then."

The one thing you need to know about modern philosophy is that the operative word in the previous sentence is "best." The first thing we had to do in that class was figure out what it meant. Was it what the person in the bed said she wanted, what the doctor wanted, what the hospital's risk manager wanted, what the church (whatever church it was) wanted, what the husband wanted, what the other doctor wanted, what the wife wanted, what the parents wanted, what the partner wanted, what the children wanted? Sorting out what was best was, to say the least, challenging. For guidance, we read works by Kant and Aristotle and Bentham that were harder to get through than the textbooks on human anatomy and organic chemistry, and, for my students, who were itching to get into the clinic, largely beside the point. While I didn't think for a minute that an abstract principle, like

Kant's categorical imperative, say, was actually going to lead to the right decision on whether or not to give a new heart to a homeless man, it seemed like a reasonable idea, in a place where right answers were often not as black-and-white as they might appear, to inject some of these notions into the future doctors' heads. If ideas like these could become part of their mental landscape, then in the future, confronted with that homeless man, they might see the terrain with greater definition.

Historically, when people looked for guidance on how to conduct their lives, they turned to philosophy or religion or both. That's less true now, as formal religious affiliations drop away and academic philosophy becomes more and more arcane. It's not that people are less inclined to examine their lives or to seek wisdom, it's just that they are more likely to look for it in other places: in support groups, on radio call-in shows, from life coaches, on the Internet, in books, or, in my case, inadvertently, with my dog, in a nursing home.

When Pransky and I started working at County, I expected to learn things—how could I not?—though what those things would be I had no clue. I assumed I'd learn something about old people, and about the therapeutic value of animals in a medical setting, and about myself in that setting, which was alien and not a little scary. What I found myself learning quickly sorted itself into a template that anyone with a Catholic education, especially—which would not include me—would recognize as the seven virtues: love, hope, faith, prudence, justice, fortitude, restraint.

It should be said that the Catholics didn't have a corner on virtue, in general, or on these seven in particular; they just happened to enumerate and, in a sense, popularize them, so when we think of virtue, we tend to think in sevens. But well before Catholic theologians codified their list, Greek philosophers, most notably Plato and Aristotle, offered advice as to the traits and behaviors that should be cultivated in order to live a good, productive, meaningful life, a life with and for others. It was to Plato's original four—courage, wisdom, justice, and restraint—that, centuries later, Saint Augustine added love, hope, and faith—what are commonly called "the theological virtues." These, he believed, both came from God and delivered one to God and, ultimately, to a place in heaven. In our own time, for most people, love and hope and even faith, if you think of it as loyalty and consistency, are unmoored from visions of an afterlife. Still, the virtues remain as guides not only to good conduct but to our better—and possibly happier, more harmonious, most humane—selves.

Happiness, as it happened, was the dominant emotion for both Pransky and me when we were at the nursing home, strange as that sounds, and strange as it was. I didn't go there to be happy any more than I did to learn about hope or fortitude, or to think about courage and faith, but that's what happened. You could say I was lucky, and, in fact, by landing at County, I was lucky. County happens to be blessed with tremendous leadership, a devoted staff, and a larger community that embraces rather than isolates it. I wouldn't presume that it is comparable to any other nursing home. But I do believe that in settings like nursing homes, as well as hospitals and hospices and any other place where life is in the balance, we get to essentials, which is what the virtues are.

More than luck was at work, too. My dog was at work, and she brought to it a lightness and easiness that seemed to expand outward and encompass almost everyone she encountered. We often talk about "getting out of our comfort zone," but rarely about entering someone else's.

Pransky made that possible. With her by my side, and sometimes in the lead, I was able to be a better, more responsive, less reticent version of myself. One day a man I didn't know was sitting idly by himself in the nursing home hall. He was wearing a badly tied hospital johnny that exposed part of his back, and nothing else. It was rare for people at County not to be dressed in street clothes, but it wasn't his attire that caught my attention. The man was jaundiced and almost as yellow as the liquid running through the tube that started under his hospital gown and ended in a bag on the side of his wheelchair. That, and he had no legs. This was not Joe, another double amputee who became one of our regulars and will appear in these pages, but someone I'd never seen before and never saw again. If I had been alone, I might have nodded in his direction and kept going, because that man represented most of the things that scared me about nursing homes: debilitating illness, a lack of privacy, bodily fluids. But I was not alone, and my partner veered in his direction, which meant that I had no choice but to go over and talk to him. What a nice guy! We talked dogs (he had two Yorkies at home), sports (he was a Steelers fan), and dogs some more. I was in his comfort zone, and Pransky's, and then, ultimately, mine. It was, in the scheme of things, a small thing, but small things add up.

My mommy would like your doggie," a youngish woman with developmental disabilities said to me the first time we met her at County.

"My doggie would like your mommy," I said. "Where does she live?"

"In heaven," she said.

"Oh," I said. "Pransky has a lot of friends in heaven." And after what was by then a year at County, it was true.

A certain amount of death is inevitable in a nursing home. This is where the virtues can be helpful. They point us at what's important and valuable in life. They can offer perspective and frames of reference, and if a dog is in the frame, all the better.

As I was working on this book, and friends asked me what it was about, I would say "right living and dogs" or "moral philosophy and dogs" or "old people and dogs." Eventually I realized that every one of those descriptions was wrong. I was saying "dogs," plural, when it was actually about one singular, faithful, charitable, loving, and sometimes prudent dog. That dog has risen from her slumber and is standing behind me now, showing great hope, restraint, and fortitude as she waits for me to stop typing and go for a walk.

1.

Restraint

As long as we're talking about virtues and dogs, let me say at the outset that we cheated. Pransky, the seven-year-old canine in question, had grown up at the end of a dirt road in Vermont where leashes were as rare as winters were long. There was one hanging on a peg somewhere in the mudroom under a scrum of fleece, Gore-Tex, and down, where it stayed for months on end. Most mornings I'd open the back porch door and Pranny would go outside and wander through our meadow, taking stock of the comings and goings of whatever voles and rabbits and turkeys and deer and coyotes and moose might have trespassed the perimeter in the night. Then, satisfied, she'd bound up the stairs, give a friendly bark, come inside, get a biscuit, and go back to bed.

Afternoons she'd ask for company, coming to the threshold of my office and staring at my back until I turned around and said something conciliatory, like, "Okay, you win." If the words weren't comprehensible, the tone was, and she'd start wagging and wagging, her entire rear end oscillating, so pleased was she that her telepathic magic had worked yet again. Soon, as she obviously knew, we'd be going down the road, she in the lead, charging with inexplicable purpose into the bordering woods, emerging yards ahead, where she'd wait until I had almost caught up. Then she'd take off again, her dog tags chinking, a low-rent GPS that let me know, always, where she was.

I'd wanted to buy one of those pretty designer leashes embroidered with paw prints, polka dots, and flowers in bright reds and happy plaids that I saw at the store, but what was the point? Pretty leashes were for dogs from somewhere else; they were for city dogs and suburban dogs and dogs that lived near traffic. And, anyhow, I wanted to believe that self-control could be stronger than any piece of nylon or leather clipped to a collar, so that if I trained this dog well, she would not need to be tethered.

When the thirteenth-century theologian Saint Thomas Aquinas named restraint as one of the cardinal virtues, what he was really talking about were certain signature human excesses, like gluttony and lust. Aquinas was riffing on Aristotle's list of virtues, themselves inherited from Plato, in which restraint also figured. Still, if you wanted to read Aristotle's list through the most literal lens, you might be able to convince yourself it applied to animals as well as people since, as the nineteenth-century scholar Thomas Marshall points out, Aristotle "defines self-restraint as good conduct with regard to those desires which are necessary to the *animal* kingdom."

But why bother? Why not just read dog-obedience books instead? Books with titles like *Control Unleashed: Creating a Focused and Confident Dog*. Books written by monks or by dog whisperers or by trainers who swore by food rewards or trainers who forswore food for little metal clickers. If they had nothing else in common, these experts, they were all writing about temperance, too. It's a Saturday afternoon and my husband, Bill, and I are sorting through the random pile of dog-training books off-loaded by friends who have been through this. He reads aloud from one that focuses on dogs as pack animals. "This one says that she won't be happy until she knows that we humans are alpha to her beta." He speaks with the authority of a convert who has found religion: "What we have to do is push her to the ground and lie on her with all of our weight when she does something wrong so she knows who is boss," he says. The progressive parent in me recoils. Our eight-year-old daughter goes to a Quaker camp and a school where everyone is a winner. I've got two shelves of parenting books with some combination of the words "reason," "happy," "resilient," "talk," and "positive" in the title. Is it any wonder that I want Pransky to listen because she trusts and respects me, not because I can throw her to the ground?

Then, by chance, a copy of Temple Grandin's book *Animals in Translation* arrived in the mail. Grandin was famous for being both a high-functioning autistic and a gifted zoologist, and her premise was that her autism put her in a unique position to serve as an intermediary between animals and humans because "autism is a kind of way station on the road from animals to humans." It was not a dog book per se—in fact, Grandin spent more

words on hogs and cows than on hounds and shepherds—
but no matter. So much of what she was saying seemed to
be universal, and when it was not, it just made sense.
("Leash laws may be short-circuiting some core principle
of animal behavior in the wild" was one bit of wisdom I
particularly liked, since it validated our habit of letting
our dog run free on our property.)

Almost as an aside, Grandin wrote about the necessity
of holding a dog when it was a puppy and touching it all
over so it would get used to intimacy with humans, and
also of taking care to look the puppy in the eye and hold
its gaze—a kind of words without words, though she also
pointed out that a dog's capacity for language was much
larger than we'd imagined. Grandin was totally in the
alpha-person/beta-dog camp, but totally against the
throw-the-dog-on-her-back-and-lie-on-top-of-her school
of making that happen. "The best ways to establish domi-
nance are obedience training and making the dog sit qui-
etly before he is fed," she counseled. Inadvertently I had
stumbled on the most useful book on dog training ever.

Pranny was then ten weeks old. She weighed, at most,
fifteen pounds. The offspring of a yellow Lab named
Sunshine and an apricot poodle called Sir Andre, she

looked like neither. She was a wavy blonde with velvet ears the color of a perfectly toasted marshmallow that were so long they dragged on the floor like a pair of pants that needed to be hemmed. Her eyes were brown and eager, and set below a pair of bushy eyebrows that made her look wise and professorial, even when she was curled in Bill's sneaker, where she liked to sleep, her purple belly (an excellent sign, according to Grandin, something to do with melanin and the mid-brain and good behavior) spilling over the side. She had a beard and dainty paws. Her tail was long and bony and waiting to feather out.

Every dog, especially every puppy, is a tabula rasa, a blank slate, on which humans seek to write. What else is obedience training but the attempt to bend a dog's will to our own? We tell them to "sit" and "stay" at our command. We demand that they "shake" by putting out a paw every time we ask—so it's not really asking, it's telling. This goes beyond teaching them behaviors that could, arguably, be called simple good manners. We also want them to have particular personalities: cuddly, say, or independent, or submissive, as if personality could be taught. We look for breed traits (even in mutts like Pranny) that suit us—docile, water-loving, athletic, child-friendly—the way we look for mates on Internet dating sites. We want the dog to be "ours" and believe, after fifteen thousand years of domestication, that it is within our power to make that happen.

Pransky was a dog who came, it seemed, out of nowhere. We had had a dog, and that dog died, and this dog was offered to us just weeks later. She was two months old, and in northern Virginia, and by chance Bill would be in Baltimore in a few days' time, and we had to decide, right then, did we want her? I was ambivalent. It was too soon. But then there were the words of my daughter, which seemed so true when she said them after Barley, our beloved twelve-year-old golden retriever, died: "This family doesn't feel right without a dog." So Bill drove over from Maryland and picked up this new puppy and brought her back in a soft-sided carrier that looked like a handbag. It was after midnight when he got home and we sat on the edge of Sophie's bed and pulled her from sleep with the words "Our new dog is here." In the morning, she thought she had dreamed it. It was October. We named the puppy Pransky, my grandmother's maiden name, because of the spritely way she walked and because in a few weeks' time the snow would fall and the woods would whiten, and we hoped to have our new dog by our side as we ventured out on skis.

Did we teach Pransky to love snow, or was she born with a mind for winter? At six months, when she weighed at most thirty pounds and stood on all fours with a foot of undercarriage clearance, our puppy went out for her first ski—six miles through soft snow that continued to fall for the few hours she trotted along. The dog whisperers would have been appalled, claiming that a young dog's body is too underdeveloped to withstand a trip like that, and it's true, when she came inside she took a long drink of water and lay on the sheepskin by the fire and fell into a deep sleep. But a few hours later, when she heard us pulling on our boots again, she jumped up and stood by the door, wagging expectantly. She was ready to go. She was always ready to go. Soon enough she learned the word "ski," and later "s-k-i," just as, in the spring, she assimilated "hike" and "walk" and "stroll" and "run" and "bike" and any noun that followed her favorite verb: "go."

But before she got "go," she had to master "come." It was imperative for a dog who would be allowed to wander leashlessly. My guide, Temple Grandin, having written eloquently about the virtues of being off-leash, did not, nonetheless, offer any advice about training a dog to behave as if the leash were there, just invisible. But maybe that was the whole point of obedience training—its end goal was a dog that came when you called because it felt the tug of your connection.

Grandin did, though, write about the sensory ways in which a dog apprehends the world, its multidimensional sense of smell, which gave me the idea of "talking" to Pranny through her nose. At the grocery store I bought pungent cheese and fragrant beef jerky. At home I opened the door, let Pransky out, waited for her to get part of the way across the meadow, then waved the jerky through the air as if it were the magic wand I wanted it to be. In a minute or so, because she either caught the scent of the meat or noticed me flapping my hand back and forth, she looked up. "Pranny, come!" I called. She seemed to be considering the proposition. All of a sudden, a switch flipped and she came charging toward me. "Good come!" I praised her, handing over a small piece of the jerky strip. We kept doing this, over and over, and before week's end her vocabulary had absorbed "come," and we moved on from smelly-food rewards to dog biscuits when she arrived, panting, at the porch door. Pretty soon she knew the word "biscuit," too.

So many words. I had never known a dog who could so easily learn and remember human spoken language. We worked on nouns first, then verbs, then nouns and verbs together. "Ball," "toy," "bone," "bed," then "get the ball," "drop the toy," "find the bone," "go to bed." After a while, when she started to take advantage of a word's essential elasticity, which is to say when I'd say "go to bed" and she'd jump up on my bed, we moved on to pronouns, specifically the second-person singular possessive pronoun. "Go to your bed," I'd say, and she'd jump down from mine and settle into hers with a quiet but audible sigh—a dog equivalent, I decided, of rolling her eyes.

We were developing our own pidgin sign language, too. Arm extended with palm out, the universal stop sign, meant *stay*. Hands moving upward together was "stand up!" Arms crossed was "lie down." Finger on lips meant "lie down," "be quiet," "be patient," "no more 360-degree turns," "we really are going out the door as soon as I tie my sneakers." At some point she seemed to understand that a finger to the lips was a finger that could not tie a shoe—if only for a minute or two.

n 1988, about fourteen years before Sunshine got together with Sir Andre in Virginia, a breeder at Guide Dogs Victoria in Australia named Wally Conron came up with the idea of crossing a Labrador retriever and a poodle to create a service dog with the friendly temperament of a Lab and the intelligence and non-shedding hair of a poodle. This last attribute was key: these could be guide dogs for people with allergies. The cross was so popular that people around the world started to have Labradoodle puppies shipped to them from Australia. Then breeders in other countries started to "make" this kind of dog. Pretty soon, with poodles as the go-to sire dog, there were goldendoodles, cockapoos, Airedoodles, bich-poos, bassetoodles, shih-poos. The draw seemed to be smart, adorable, non-shedding.

We got Pransky, though, because she was a failure: she shed. The family that was supposed to take her home couldn't, because of this. So we were prepared for dog hair on the furniture and on our clothes, and we were prepared for a cute little animal—we had seen the pictures. We assumed she'd be smart, too. Even so, her intelligence and eagerness to learn caught us by surprise. She seemed always to be waiting for a new assignment.

If a human brain is plastic—able to change through learning—so must a dog's be. The common refrain that "you can't teach an old dog new tricks" began to seem like an excuse for human laziness. Why couldn't dogs learn throughout their lives, like we could? How could there be a switch for learning that one day turned off and stayed off? Maybe it was just a matter of not stopping at "sit," "stay," "come."

I tried. She tried. I bought toys. She learned to distinguish between the stuffed bear and the stuffed bone. But after a few years of this, long past "find your sock and bring it inside," Pranny was bored. She'd pretend sleep, eyes closed, ears open, listening for any sound of an activity that might include her. I'd stand up from my desk and she'd jump up from wherever she was in the house and report, at the ready, by my side. Too bad we were only going downstairs to fold the laundry. It was pretty clear to me that she needed a job.

But what? We didn't have sheep, so she couldn't be a herding dog. We didn't hunt, even though she did at times, trotting home with a still-warm bunny or squirrel. Could she, though, go back to her roots and become a service dog? The original Labradoodle was a seeing eye dog; Pransky, at six, was too old for that, and anyhow, I wasn't willing to give her over to someone else. There are all sorts of service dogs: search-and-rescue dogs, cancer-sniffing dogs, paratrooper dogs, mobility dogs, seizure-alert dogs, hearing dogs, but most of these are full-time occupations not suitable for a family pet. Even so, I read all the descriptions like an unemployed person studying the classifieds. "Pranny," I'd ask my reclining canine, stretched out on the couch, "would you like to be a bomb-sniffer dog?" She thumped her tail. "Pranny, do you want to be a Navy Seal dog and jump out of airplanes?" More thumps. "Are you sure? You'd have to eat MREs." Extra thumps—"eat" was one of her words. "Should we get some sheep?"

The therapy dog description was different. It was like reading a classified that had our names on it, one that said "Wanted: irresistibly cute blond dog with a black olive nose and distinctive eyebrows who is friendly to all, kind, enthusiastic, well behaved, smart, and willing to spend time with people who could use some love and affection. Jumpers and barkers need not apply. Must have a loyal human partner who need not be anywhere near as attractive." It was perfect! We were there!

Then I read the requirements to become a certified therapy dog team. We would have to pass a test composed of fifteen different tasks. Fail any one of them and that was that. It seemed overwhelming and hard. I printed out the testing brochure and put it aside. And then, as these things go, it got lost in the shuffle.

A full year later, it resurfaced. By then Pranny was nearly seven, Bill was traveling the world for work, and our teenage daughter, Sophie, was about to go away to school. With mom's taxi service going out of business I'd have a lot more free time, so I read through the testing requirements more keenly, wondering: Were we ready, Pransky and I, to become a therapy dog team? Did we have what it took? Well, no and no. But could we? Maybe. Possibly. Pranny, at least, was built for this.

The first requirement was that Pransky would have to prove she was "accepting of a friendly stranger," which of course she was, greeting with exuberant waggling everyone who knocked on our door, and soon returning with a gift of one of her prized socks or stuffed animals or marrow bones in her mouth. The problem was, this was not what Therapy Dogs International (TDI) had in mind. "The evaluator and handler shake hands and exchange pleasantries," the requirements brochure said. "The dog must show no sign of resentment or shyness, and must not break position or try to go to the evaluator." This was going to be challenging. Indifference was not in Pransky's DNA.

I was pretty sure she would have no trouble with the second requirement, though—"sitting politely for petting"—especially since there was a dispensation for dogs that stood when the evaluator petted them, or number three, "appearance and grooming," or number seven, "coming when called." After these, my confidence waned. Pransky would also have to demonstrate that she was able to (number five) walk through a crowd without expressing any interest in passersby; (number six) sit down and stay while the handler walked twenty feet ahead; (number eight) show "no more than a casual interest in other dogs"; (number nine) be impervious to distractions, like joggers passing by; (number ten) not get spooked by wheelchairs and walkers; (number eleven) walk by a plate of food on the floor and pretend not to be interested; (number twelve) be comfortable around people who were wheezing or limping or moaning; (number thirteen) stay cool and collected and polite when handed off to the evaluator as the handler walked away and out of sight for a full three minutes; (number fourteen) present herself for petting to a person in a wheelchair or hospital bed; and (number fifteen) be calm and low-key around children—even running, squealing children.

You might have noticed that I skipped requirement number four. Where all the other requirements struck me as potentially learnable and doable, number four— "out for a walk (walking on a loose leash)"—only struck fear, the fear of failure. It read: "This test demonstrates that the handler is in control of the dog. The dog can be on either side of the handler, whichever the handler prefers. There must be a left turn, a right turn, and an about turn, with at least one stop in between and another at the end. The dog need not be perfectly aligned with the handler and need not sit when the handler stops." In other words, a dog that was *so not* perfectly aligned with the handler so as to appear to be taking the handler for a walk, that dog—that pulling, straining, yanking dog—would not cut it. And that dog was mine.

Have you ever seen a dog tugging on its leash with such determination it appeared to be strangling itself?

That was Pransky. The few times she had to be leashed, she pulled so hard that she coughed hoarsely for days afterward. Clip a leash to her collar and she became a different dog, one who, inexplicably, could not figure out that she'd feel a lot better if she just relaxed. Talking to her had no effect. Treats had no effect. (Well, that's not exactly true—they'd cause her to trot back to my side, chew, and charge ahead again.) Our vet suggested we invest in a Gentle Leader, a pricey piece of nylon that slid over the snout and buckled behind the ears, halter-style, and came with a large tin button for the owner to wear that said "It's not a muzzle," which is precisely what the Gentle Leader looked like. The vet said it had cured his own dog, an inveterate puller. I handed over nearly $50, which seemed like a lot of money for a foot of nylon webbing and a couple of metal fasteners, but it also seemed like a complete bargain, since it was going to fix this problem pronto.

"When she pulls with this thing on, it puts pressure on the bridge of her nose and the back of her neck and mimics the feeling of a mother dog scolding her puppy," the vet said. "She'll stop almost immediately."

I had seen large dogs—golden retrievers and German

shepherds—strolling amiably down the streets in town with these things strapped over their noses. I was excited to bring one home and try it.

But home was half an hour's car ride away. As soon as we left the vet's office, I slipped the halter on Pranny, buckled it in the back, and attached her leash. We were going for a walk. A civilized walk. Our first, ever. I took a step forward and, miracle of miracles, Pransky stepped forward and did not pull. So far, so good. I took another step. Pranny moved forward, too, then lay down and tried to wrestle the halter off with her paws. I scolded her and she stood up. A family walked by and a girl who looked about seven asked if she could pet my dog. I was about to say "Of course," when the mother, looking alarmed, asked why the dog was wearing a muzzle. "It's not a muzzle," I said, adding: "It's to prevent pulling," but they had moved on. I took another step forward. Pranny did, too, only this time she dragged her snout on the ground, trying to get the halter off that way. It was a trick worthy of Houdini, and it took all of two minutes before the Gentle Leader was hanging from her neck and she was free. I put it back on, tighter this time. She dropped her snout to the ground again and nose-surfed. It looked painful.

The whole halter concept was a crutch, anyway. That, at least, was what the therapy dog testing brochure implied. "Dogs must be tested on a plain buckle collar or harness," it said. "Training collars, training harnesses, halties, or any other corrective training devices are not permitted during testing or visiting as a TDI-registered therapy dog." Dogs that could not walk politely on a regular leash-and-collar setup, the nameless writer suggested, did not have what it took to work in the public sphere. And a dog that couldn't walk politely even with a training device? This was so beneath consideration it didn't warrant mention.

Desperate, I consulted Google. I was looking for advice, for behavioral tips, for anything that was going to help my dog learn to walk with a restraint as if it weren't there. One person said that all I had to do was walk in one direction till the dog pulled, then do an immediate about-face and walk in that direction till the dog pulled, then do an about-face and walk in that direction till the dog pulled, then do an about-face and walk in that direction till the dog pulled . . . and on and on. For us it meant, essentially, walking in a dizzying circle. Another claimed that the surefire way to break the pulling habit was to stop walking as soon as the leash went taut—stop, and stand there, and wait. Then, once the leash went slack, we could start walking again. This writer claimed that as soon as a dog understood that a loose leash meant "go" and a tight leash meant "stop," the dog would stop pulling. But, the writer cautioned, this could mean standing still for ten minutes at a time or more, with "or more" being the operative words for Pran and me.

It was early June. The mosquitoes were biting wherever the blackflies had missed. The certification test I was aiming for was on the last day of August, just three months away. Our routine changed with this in mind. Now when Pranny came to get me for our afternoon stroll, I'd fill my pockets with dog biscuits, attach the leash to her collar, and go outside for our "walk." After years of running free, this must have seemed like an affront to her, and certainly weird, but not as weird as what came next: we didn't go anywhere. Seven paces out, with barely enough time for me to say "slow walking," Pranny was at one end of a stretched leash and I was at the other. I'd stop. She'd stop. (More accurately, I'd stop and she'd jerk back a little before coming to a stop.) And while sometimes she'd look over her shoulder to query me about our lack of progress, she didn't stop straining: the leash was still straight out and so was my arm. The minutes would tick by, the mosquitoes would swarm, and the blackflies would congregate on the back of my neck. This wasn't a test of wills, it was a test of will—mine. Pransky, my very smart dog, just didn't get it. She appeared to have no clue that we'd move forward as soon as she stopped pulling.

When I couldn't take it anymore (and yes, I knew, as any parent who has had to Ferberize her baby, that inconsistency was the hobgoblin of little minds), I'd pat my pocket and call Pranny to my side, and she'd come back happily, expectantly, and I'd give her a biscuit for coming. With the leash slack again, we'd continue our walk, go seven paces, stop, wait, get hammered by the bugs, wait some more, and more, and more, and then I'd give in. Twenty minutes and we were still at the top of the driveway.

We soldiered on. Some days were less bad than others. Some days she even seemed to be catching on to the concept of "slow walking" and "no pull." The clock was ticking. June became July. Deerflies supplanted blackflies. And though Pranny and I were now marking progress in feet, not inches, it was pretty clear that we were going to bomb. Asking my dog, whose whole experience of the outdoors was, until this point in her life, unfettered and carefree, who would sniff the air for messages and signs and then go running off to decipher them— asking her to amble slowly on a leash was like asking her to walk by a juicy porterhouse steak as if it weren't there. Which, of course, was part of the test, too. A therapy dog had to respond to the command "leave it!" even when every sensory neuron in her body was shouting "steal it, swipe it, run under the couch, and devour it!" Gluttony, the vice that first got Aristotle thinking about temperance and restraint, had no place in the emotional repertoire of a therapy dog.

Six weeks into our training, when failure seemed assured, I made a call to the local nursing home. It was a feint, a fake to the right. I told the volunteer coordinator that I'd recently published a book about dementia, and had spent some time with dementia patients at hospitals on both coasts, and wanted to bring my incredibly well-behaved dog into her dementia unit to work with her patients. I hoped she'd jump at the opportunity to have us there, knocking aside the ever-narrowing hoop of therapy dog certification, which would then roll away, out of sight. I was also counting on the "fact" that no one spends time in a nursing home unless they must, so of course she'd welcome us. We've all seen the pictures and read the stories about how nursing homes warehouse the elderly, about patients tied to their beds, about the odors of urine and putrefaction, because what are nursing homes but the place where death lives? Hospitals, with their operating rooms and antibiotics and defibrillators and tubes and wires, seem more hopeful by an order of magnitude.

The volunteer coordinator passed me along to the activities director, a woman I'll call Janie, just as I'll call everyone at that place by a different name in the interest of confidentiality. I told her about Pransky, dropping adjectives like "cute" and "calm" and "friendly" and "cute" and "sweet" and "gentle" and "cute."

"She does sound cute," Janie said. "I'm sure she'd be great." Hearing no hesitation in her voice, I was already looking forward to leash-free afternoon jaunts through the woods with my dog again.

"Which therapy dog organization are you affiliated with?" Janie asked.

I explained that we were "in process with TDI."

"Good," she said. "As soon as you have your documentation, we'd be happy to have you. We like cute dogs."

Thwarted, I tried my last gambit: "We want to work in the memory-care wing," I said, and explained that I'd had some experience and that I'd written a book, hoping that my implied expertise would overcome her allegiance to protocol, and that this would be the key that turned the lock that let us in.

To be honest, there was another reason why I wanted to be assigned to the dementia unit: it scared me less. The paradox of Alzheimer's disease and other dementias is that as devastating as they are, their victims typically don't look sick until the end. In my mind's caricature of what I'll call the County Nursing Home and Rehabilitation Center, the general population languished in their rooms while the dementia patients were sequestered behind locked doors so they wouldn't wander away, with the key word being "wander." These patients were ambulatory. They were not confined to bed. They got dressed every day. They were confused, yes, and yes, they were desperately ill, but even so, appearances were deceiving, and I was happy to be deceived. At the same time, I was counting on other people being unnerved by people with serious memory loss, so that wanting to spend time with these people would get us extra credit.

"Wow!" Janie said cheerfully. "That's amazing." I was back to feeling encouraged. "You're like the fifth person this month who wants to volunteer in the special-care unit." I was back to feeling discouraged.

"But no one else has a dog." I was feeling encouraged again.

"The thing is," Janie said, "the special-care unit already has a therapy animal, a cat who lives there."

"Pransky loves cats," I said, which may not have been a lie. I had no idea. She had never met a cat. She definitely liked small rodents, which she'd chase through our meadow and sometimes even catch.

"Oh, and there's a therapy dog that visits sometimes, too," Janie added. "But we'd love to have you two work with our general patient population. They haven't had a therapy dog in a long time. That's where we could really use help. Let's set up a time for you to go through orientation—it takes a couple of hours—so as soon as you and Pransky get your certification you can start."

And so, to recap: not only had I agreed to work with

the old folks at County, there would be no shortcuts to get there. It was back to "slow-walking" for Pranny and me.

There are very good and crucial reasons to go through therapy dog training and get certified. I knew this even while I was trying to bypass the process. Insurance, for one, since official therapy dogs come with liability insurance that covers both members of the team while they're on duty. The other reason is safety: while to the untrained eye a nursing home may be a hotbed of lassitude, almost everything that goes on there is an accident waiting to happen—people moving slowly, pushing walkers; people breathing with oxygen, tethered to a tank; people undergoing physical therapy in the hallway; people with bad backs who want to bend over to pet your dog—and to whatever extent possible, you want to know that your dog knows how to behave, and that it will listen to you and instantly obey your commands. The communication between human and animal is vital, which is why you get certified as a team. My dog may understand commands and gestures, and she may know precisely what to do when she and I are working together, but this does not necessarily translate to her responding to anyone but me. A therapy dog team is like a pair of dance partners, able to anticipate each other's moves and read body language and pick up on the most subtle cues. That's why Pransky, standing at the threshold of my office with her face to my back, did not have to do anything for me to know what she wanted, and why she knew that as long as she remained there she would be "saying" the same thing. No barking, no whining, nothing more than the whoosh of air as her tail tocked in anticipation, waiting for the pen to drop, the phone to be returned to its cradle, or certain words spoken to confirm what she wanted to be true—that we were going outside.

And so we continued our peculiar pas de deux. It wasn't graceful. It wasn't balletic. It wasn't fun. But I had started to think about those people at County. Many of them had grown up on farms and missed the companionship of animals, Janie had told me. A friendly dog would, if even for a short time, bring them a sense of home. I found myself consulting the testing brochure regularly, as if it were a recipe and I might have forgotten an ingredient. Before long even the tests that seemed at the outset to be slam-dunks were starting to feel like three-pointers from half-court. Grooming, for instance, wasn't just a matter of looking good. The dog had to let the tester run a brush through her hair, lift up her earflaps, examine her paws. As a puppy, Pranny had had chronic ear infections, and though her ears had healed, the infections had left her skittish: if anyone other than a family member so much as glanced at her ears, she'd yelp reflexively. "It's psychological," we'd explain to startled friends and strangers as they'd pull back, aghast at the pain they thought they'd inflicted. Would the tester be so forgiving?

n the beginning, there were no testers and no tests. In the beginning, which was sometime during World War II, in the Pacific, there was a small, stray Yorkshire terrier that was adopted by an American soldier, Corporal William Wynne, who called her Smoky. Smoky accompanied Wynne and his mates into battle, and kept them company under fire and back at camp. When Wynne fell ill, his friends brought Smoky to the hospital, where she cheered up the other patients as well as her master. By chance, the physician in charge was Dr. Charles Mayo, of the Mayo Clinic, who recognized the dog's therapeutic value and allowed her to stay, even letting Smoky sleep in Wynne's bed. What he seemed to know, intuitively, was that when we invite dogs into our world, they change it, and we change, too. What he did not know and could not have anticipated was that the feedback loop encircling this particular pair would expand outward and grow ever and ever wider, until it encompassed tens of thousands of people and dogs, two of whom were now Pransky and me.

For the longest time, evidence that therapy dogs were having a beneficial effect on hospital and nursing home patients was largely anecdotal; most of the early studies of dogs in medical settings looked at whether they were vectors of parasites and bacteria and seemed to start from the premise that animals did not belong among the infirm. The hard science of dogs as healers has come more recently. In one study, researchers measured the anxiety levels of 230 hospitalized psychiatric patients after a routine therapy session and after an animal-assisted one and found "statistically significant reductions in anxiety scores . . . after the animal-assisted therapy . . . for patients with psychotic disorders, mood disorders, and other [psychiatric] disorders." Another study, this one of people undergoing complete joint replacement, found that patients visited by therapy dogs required half as much pain medication as patients who did not have any animal assistance. More recently, the Mars Corporation, the people who bring us M&M's and Kit Kats, pledged $2 million to help underwrite the National Institutes of Health's effort to understand the role dogs can play in the lives of the autistic. Meanwhile, the U.S. Army has spent $300,000 to study the ameliorating effects of therapy dogs on veterans with post-traumatic stress disorder—a number of whom are now training dogs to work with other veterans with PTSD.

That first veteran therapy dog, Smoky, continued visiting hospital patients for twelve postwar years. Clearly no one cared if she was a good leash walker or knew to ignore food dropped on the floor. Smoky was skilled at what she did. It was a good quarter of a century before anyone thought to come up with rules and regulations for therapy dogs or to buy insurance to cover what might happen when they were on duty, but once they did, therapy dog organizations sprang up all over the world. Some were specific to a country, a region, or a state; some were specific to a particular kind of therapy; some used the American Kennel Association's Good Citizenship program as a jumping-off point; some made up their own rules. TDI, the organization whose requirements we were training to meet, would give us the option of working all across the country and abroad. Not that I was planning on this. But as long as we were spending so much time *not* walking down the driveway, the idea of working in the wide world was appealing.

As hard as it was, the training was paying off in ways I hadn't anticipated. Just the idea that there was a test in our future kept me focused, the way a 10K in April keeps a runner slogging through slush in March. The "professional" designation—the special red therapy dog bandanna, official ID card, and yellow tag that Pransky and I would earn—was also motivating. As much as they were like the T-shirt and tacky ribbon handed out at the end of that 10K, they were more than that, too, though maybe my sense that they were more was really about how difficult they were to obtain; there was no limping to the finish line. But the training made what we were hoping to do—work in a nursing home—real to me, since it forced me to think ahead to the challenges we might face. Without this, the people we'd be spending time with were just stock characters from a story I was making up. I had been to County once, for a total of fifteen minutes, to drop off a radio for an ailing relative of a friend of mine. I knew nothing.

Nor was I alone in my ignorance. Around the same time Pransky and I were in training, the Pew Research Center conducted a survey of nearly three thousand people to find out how young and middle-aged adults imagine old age, and how the elderly actually experience it. What the researchers found was that there was a significant gap between the two. "These disparities come into sharpest focus when survey respondents are asked about a series of negative benchmarks often associated with aging, such as illness, memory loss, an inability to drive, an end to sexual activity, a struggle with loneliness and depression, and difficulty paying bills," the Pew researchers wrote. "In every instance, older adults report experiencing [these benchmarks] at lower levels (often far lower) than younger adults report expecting to encounter them when they grow old."

People talk about how, in our culture especially, we do not know how to deal with the inevitable fact that we will die, and how, instead of accepting it, we medicalize death, trying to make it into something that can be treated, as if it were a disease, as if it were surmountable.

In 2010 Medicare paid $55 billion—more than the budgets for the Department of Homeland Security or the Department of Education—for doctor and hospital bills during the last two months of patients' lives, and about a third of the treatment they paid for had no meaningful effect. As the Pew study suggested, it's not just death we're struggling with, it's what comes before death as well. And because younger people are now largely insulated from older people, who pliantly congregate in enclaves called retirement communities and assisted living facilities, if not in nursing homes, old age, dying, and death are so removed from everyday life that they seem alien and strange and avoidable. Until they are not.

The County Nursing Home and Rehabilitation Center was at the far end of town, the last building in a residential neighborhood that segued into fields and farmland. It was a friendly-enough-looking place, a single-story brick building that resembled an elementary school, with one wing off to the left, one wing off to the right, and a third section connecting them. Flower beds ringed the circular drive, their yellow mums and orange lilies sitting at the top of mulch mounds that were fresh and well tended. If they had enough time for groundskeeping, I thought, maybe the patients weren't so bad off, either. I pushed through the front door and stepped into the foyer. The place was eerily quiet; the receptionist booth was empty; not a soul seemed to be around. I took a cautious breath and smelled . . . roses. Someone had left a bouquet in a vase on a coffee table near the entrance. Nearby was a hand-sanitizer dispenser and a sign that stressed the importance of taking precautions not to bring germs in or out, so I loaded up on the foam, rubbing my hands over and over, hoping that if someone were to walk by, they'd see that I was taking things seriously. No one did. I took a chance and followed what sounded like a French accent down the hall, into a room on the opposite side of the corridor, and peeked inside. Fifteen older adults in wheelchairs were arrayed around an oversized TV watching *The Pink Panther*. It was the original with Peter Sellers, not the remake with Steve Martin. Or not watching—most of them were asleep, their heads flopped forward or leaning askew on their necks. As I stood there, a younger woman—younger in this instance meaning in her forties—emerged from a back office, saw me, and said, "Oh my gosh!" and stuck out her hand and introduced herself. "Crazy day," she said. Janie was short, had light brown hair cut in a kind of pageboy, with bangs that fell over a pair of chunky brown glasses. Her face was open, her smile sheepish. "I'm glad you found us," she said.

Janie walked me across the hall, to a boxy room that was filled with Formica tables and just a few chairs, over-looking the parking lot, and sat me down in front of an old television set. She slid a tape—the old-fashioned VHS kind—into a VCR, apologized because she had to rush off to a meeting, and said she'd be back in an hour, when the orientation video would be over. I was all by myself in a corner of this cavernous room, wondering what I was doing there, wondering if the old people I'd just seen would be the people Pranny and I would be vis-iting, and if they were, if they'd be sleepy then, too, and if they were, what was the point? The person on the video kept repeating himself. The basic message was: do not do anything for a patient without first consulting a nurse. Even fulfilling a simple request for water could put a patient in danger; water could be aspirated. Oh, and don't call them patients, call them residents; when you entered their room, you were entering their home.

When the video ended I filled out a form that said I understood what I had watched and was comfortable with the rules. Janie had left a copy of the volunteer handbook, too, so I read through it, cover to cover, while I waited for her to come back. "Volunteers should not invite confidences," it said. "Volunteers should never offer opinions on personal affairs, medical treatment, or choice of physician." As I sat there, workers started coming out of what I guessed was the kitchen to fill a steam table at the other end of the room and to lay tablecloths and cutlery in preparation for lunch. Janie rushed back in and led me to a nurses' station where, in two seconds, a taciturn nurse put a needle in my arm, pulled it out, and told me I'd need to get it "read" in three days to make sure I didn't have tuberculosis.

"You'd be surprised at how many people, when they know you work here, ask you about a particular resident and how they're doing," Janie cautioned as I sat in the windowless closet of an office she shared with a part-time chaplain and the other two members of her staff. She handed me another form to sign, this one agreeing to a criminal background check. "You have to say 'I'm not sure, but I'm sure they'd love a visit from you.' Or people will stop you at the store and ask you if so-and-so is still in the nursing home, and if they do, you can't tell them. The only time I've ever had to dismiss a volunteer was because of confidentiality." I nodded, but I could easily see myself slipping and telling my neighbor that I'd just seen her old boss in here—which I had. He was being pushed down the hallway to the lunchroom as I was being taken to the nurses' station to get the TB test. And now I couldn't tell her.

"There's chicken and biscuits for lunch, if you want to stay," Janie said, standing up. I didn't. What I wanted to do was to go home and slow walk the dog. The test was nineteen days away.

Agway, where we bought Pransky's food, had a big sign out front saying it was dog-friendly, so a week before the big day I took her there to see how she'd do in the real world —the world of lawn tractors, gas grills, peonies, pesticides, compost, flannel shirts, seed potatoes, suet, and shoppers. The two of us walked up the main aisle, past sacks of peat moss and rows of puddle boots, and as we did, people would stop what they were doing, reach down, and give the dog a pat, sometimes stopping to talk to her, too. She didn't exactly make eye contact, but she didn't shy away, either. We made our way from the seed racks to the potting soil through a cacophony of smells shouting out to her nose. As we walked, Pranny kept looking up at me, unsure of what was expected, trying to read my face. I kept up a quiet patter to reassure her, telling her what we were going to do, and that she was a good dog, and letting her know that, yes, I was in charge.

We stopped in the dog food section, where forty-pound bags of Fit & Trim and California Natural towered over both of us and open bins filled to the brim with crisp, dried pig ears, rawhide chews, and dog biscuits sat at precisely dog-mouth height. It was a test in self-control. At any moment, Pransky could reach in and commit larceny. "Leave it!" I said prophylactically. Loudly, too. A shopper studying the ingredients on a can of food for dogs with poultry allergies looked up, scowled at me, and then smiled winningly at my dog, as if to say that if Pransky were her dog, she would not be leading a life of denial.

"Therapy dog," I explained. "In training."

"That's nice, hon," the woman said, putting the can back on the shelf and moving on.

I walked Pransky over to the cat food aisle and dropped the leash.

"Pransky," I commanded, "sit."

Pransky sat.

"Pransky," I said, folding my arms, "lie down."

She lay down.

"Pransky," I said, a little louder this time, "stay!" I held out my hand, palm out, as if I were a traffic cop. "Stay!" I said again, looking her in the eyes, holding her gaze. Then I turned abruptly and, taking my time, walked to the far end of the aisle. When I turned around, she was still lying there.

"Pransky," I said for the last time, "come!" I clapped my hands. She stood up and ran to my side.

If there were a test for retail therapy dogs, she would have passed right then.

Two days to go, and still aiming for real-world experiences, I took Pransky to a subdivision not far from the nursing home. With kids on bikes and skateboards, parents pushing strollers, dogs barking, the whine of lawn mowers, and the whoosh of cars zipping by, I figured there would be enough distractions to throw Pransky off her game, hoping all the while that her skills were now so ingrained that her game face was on permanently. After our success at Agway I wasn't too concerned. Walking through Sunset Acres was more an exercise in redundancy than a test of expertise. We were sitting pretty.

At least Pranny was. I opened the car door and she jumped out and without a word from me sat down on the sidewalk, waiting to be leashed.

"What a good dog!" I told her, and she wagged, her tail moving last winter's sand and salt side-to-side like a windshield wiper clearing snow. "Stand up!" I commanded. She stood up. "Okay," I said, "let's go!" With that, she was off, charging ahead as if she'd forgotten that the two of us were connected.

"Slow!" I cautioned. "Slow down. Slow walk. Slow. Slow. Slow. Slow." Was she hearing "go, go, go, go?" It seemed so. She was pulling, straining to get ahead. The months melted away and we were back at the beginning of the summer, before all those training sessions in the driveway. I planted my feet and refused to go forward. A woman, a little boy holding her hand, and a slightly older boy on a Hot Wheels tricycle passed, and when Pransky turned to follow them, I seized the momentary play in the leash to move ahead again. And that was how it went, for twenty minutes or so, pulling, pulling, until I turned to go back to the car and Pransky turned, too, and proceeded to walk amiably by my side as if it were the most natural thing in the world.

When an endurance athlete trains for a marathon, she usually tapers in the days right before the race. On T minus one I abandoned the leash altogether and took Pransky for a hike on the trails behind our house. It had rained overnight, and before long she was up to her elbows in mud and my sneakers were saturated, so we detoured into the river, and my dog was happy. She raced around the woods, flushing grouse, leaping over downed trees, scrambling up hillocks. She was a dog on the last day of school. Only it wasn't the last day of school, it was the day before—or, more accurately, it was the day before the final exam, the one that would determine the semester's grade. Five miles into our hike, as Pransky began to flag and walk a step or two ahead of me and then draw even, and then drop back, I realized I knew how we would pass the test: we would cheat.

W as it cheating if the ultimate goal was honorable? Was it cheating if there was nothing self-indulgent about it? Aristotle, for one, was unclear. He seemed to be saying that there were two things that counted when you were trying to understand if the way you were behaving was virtuous: first, you needed an end that could be considered good, and second, you had to have a conscious, thoughtful, deliberate path to reach that goal. What he didn't seem to be saying was that the end justifies the means. And yet, I decided, Aristotle might approve of my plan. It involved tempering my dog's *akrasia*—Aristotle's word for what Pransky was doing when she pulled. *Akrasia* translated from the Greek as "incontinence," but it had nothing to do with bathroom habits and everything to do with excess. I was using Pransky's *akrasia* against her, just as Edward Jenner did when he sought to inoculate people against smallpox by injecting them with small doses of the disease.

At nine the next morning, seven hours before the test and four hours before we'd have to leave the house to get to the testing site—at a decommissioned Air Force base in Plattsburgh, New York—I hopped on my mountain bike. Pransky, who had followed me outside, did a pair of complete 360 turns, since the bike meant only one thing: I was going for a ride and she'd be running alongside me. Fifteen minutes and three miles later, we were back. At eleven a.m. we did the same thing. Pransky was ecstatic: two bike rides in one morning! An hour later, Sophie went for a run. Pransky tagged along. By the time we got in the car for the two-hour drive to Plattsburgh, Pransky had run at least eight miles. She was happy, and whupped. If she didn't sleep it off on the way over—which she couldn't, since I'd enlisted Sophie to keep her awake— we had a chance.

The parade ground, where the test would be held, was a massive oval in the middle of the base surrounded by identical two-story brick buildings. Off to one side, two teams of kids were squaring off on a soccer pitch, while at the far end, a Little League game was in progress. Meanwhile, about five hundred seagulls patrolled the center lawn. Though it was three in the afternoon, the sun was strong and relentless: the thermometer in my car said it was ninety-four degrees out. With an hour to kill, Pransky and I set off to walk from one end of the oval to the other. This would be our final review. On went the leash. Off went my dog. I tried to keep up with her, but the faster I went, the faster she went. Was anyone watching?

We walked for half an hour, until the heat got to us both and we retreated to the car, turned on the air-conditioning, and shared a liter of water. Through the window I could see people marking off the testing course with yellow caution tape. People with dogs were converging from all sides now, as if drawn by an inaudible whistle. We got out of the car and went toward them, passing a woman walking an Australian shepherd and tossing him treats from a rock-climbing chalk bag attached to her belt.

"Do you know—" I started.

"Please don't come closer," she said. Was her dog sick? Aggressive? She tossed him another treat. I took a step backward.

"We need to concentrate," she said tersely. "We're about to be tested. We've already failed twice." Inauspicious words, but as she spoke them, my dog sat down by my side, while her dog tried to upend the chalk bag.

I signed us in and was told we'd be the third team tested—about an hour's wait. We took off walking again, but this time Pransky was having none of it. Weariness had set in. She was hot and exhausted. Was this some sort of karmic revenge? Were we going to fail because my dog had lost her *akrasia*? Aristotle said we should aim for the golden mean. Had I pushed Pransky too far to the other side, from exuberance to disaffection? We retreated to the shade of the nearest tree and watched as the dogs ahead of us went through their paces.

When it was our turn, we walked over to the tester, an unsmiling woman who was all business in an official TDI polo shirt and a pair of black capris, and Pransky presented herself for petting. The woman bent down, inspected Pransky's paws, lifted Pransky's earflaps, and ran her fingers through Pransky's hair. If it was possible for a dog to look professional, mine did. No longer weary or bored, she was attentive and on point. Without a word, the woman clipped a long lead on Pransky's collar and instructed me to give the "stay" command, walk to the end of the lead, then turn and call my dog. It wasn't how we'd practiced it, but Pranny seemed to know what to do. She sat there, stock-still and attentive, then came trotting when I gave the call. It was such a perfect execution, it reminded me of a gymnast at the Olympics nailing a dismount, and I told her so. Then the tester put a plate of dog biscuits on the ground and asked us to walk around it, with me on the outside and Pransky not more than five inches from all that goodness. Maybe it was the weather, or maybe the biscuits were stale. Pransky circled them as if they were not there.

On it went. We walked through a crowd of people banging on pots and blowing whistles. We walked through a crowd of people in wheelchairs, people pushing walkers over the grass, people on crutches. Suddenly, without warning, the tester fell to the ground and started moaning. Heat stroke? A heart attack? I didn't know what to do, so I stood there and so did my dog. "Good!" the tester said, jumping up. "If someone falls, you do not approach with the dog, and you never try to pick them up." She looked at her clipboard and checked something off. We were in the home stretch. It was our game to lose.

"Do you see that cone over there?" the tester asked. She pointed at an orange traffic cone about forty feet away. "Please walk your dog to it, around it, and back." This was it. This was test number four, walking with a loose leash. This was every afternoon in the driveway, the mosquito bites, the blackflies. This was every ounce of restraint. I looked down at my dog. She caught my gaze as if I had tossed it to her. Her eyebrow twitched. Had she just winked?

Later, when Pransky was resting on the documents that made us legal, the tester walked by. "I can always tell the good ones," she said.

2.

Prudence

We've been waiting for you," the receptionist said, leaning over her desk, talking directly to my dog. "Welcome." It was ten a.m. on our first day at County, and it was pretty clear that no one was waiting for me. I was just the person holding the leash. In New York City, Times Square vendors sold something called "the invisible dog"—a stiff lead attached to a harness collar that could be "walked" down the street. People would notice the dog walker strolling purposefully along the sidewalk, then look down to check out the dog, and there would be none. That was Pranny and me, only reversed: we were a leash, a dog, and her imperceptible walker.

And I was relieved. The invisibility cloak that seemed to fall around my shoulders when Pransky and I crossed the threshold into County that September morning was also hiding my self-consciousness. What was I supposed to do, really? Nothing in my life had prepared me for the simple act of visiting strangers in a place like this—not the nursing home orientation video, not therapy dog training, and not, certainly, all my years in school. I was deficient in prudence, what the moral philosophers describe as "practical wisdom," the basic knowledge of what to do and how to be. There was the unsettling intimacy of visiting people in their beds, and there was the disparity between my situation and theirs: between sickness and health, between their age and mine, between confinement and freedom, between no dog and dog. And speaking of that dog, with a wag of her tail and a gentle tug on the leash, she was aiming us toward a man in the corridor beckoning to her with both his hands. Diving into the deep end, I followed.

Joe was sitting in his wheelchair. A camo-print baseball hat covered his bald head, and he wore a baggy gray sweatshirt that fell loosely to his lap, which was where, for all intents and purposes, his body ended, too. The man was all torso; his legs had been amputated at mid-thigh. I didn't want to stare, so I focused on his face, which was oriented dogward and had been hijacked by a big, goofy smile.

"Come here," he said to Pransky, with a slight slur in his voice. She drew close. Joe reached over and vigorously rubbed a spot on her head between her ears, and as he did, Pransky stuck her nose in his lap and avidly inspected his stumps, which were wrapped in flesh-colored elastic bandages. Mortified, I quickly assessed the options: pull her away and maybe make the situation worse, or do nothing and maybe make the situation worse. It was lose-lose all around. I had no idea what to do. Aristotle had convinced me that, since practical wisdom was gained by experience, the inexperienced were out of luck.

"One can learn the principles of action, but applying them in the real world, in situations one could not have foreseen, requires experience of the world," I read in a discussion of his *Nichomachean Ethics.* "For example, if one knows that one should be honest, one might act in certain situations in ways that cause pain and offense;

knowing how to apply honesty in balance with other considerations and in specific contexts requires experience." (Translation: when your best friend, who has put on a few pounds, asks if she looks fat, say no.) Was Aristotle advocating lying? Well, sort of. What he really seemed to be saying was that prudence is never black or white, and it is the wise person who figures out how to make the perfect shade of gray. Even so, in this case, the case of my sweet dog rooting around Joe's truncated limbs, there was only black or white: either I called her off or I didn't. It definitely qualified as an unforeseen situation.

"Nice dog," Joe said, beaming at Pransky. And with those words, a spell was broken. If he didn't care that she was seriously interested in his bandages, and if he was not embarrassed, why should I be embarrassed? Empathy requires us to imagine ourselves *as* someone else, but that's not what I was doing. Instead, I was putting my intact self in that wheelchair, which was not the same thing.

"How old?" Joe asked.

"Seven," I said.

He laughed—I wasn't sure why—then looked crestfallen.

"I had a dog," he said. "Lab. Hit by a car."

I was getting used to his telegraphic way of speaking in quick, simple bursts.

"Did you take him hunting?" I asked. This, I realized, was presumptuous and had to do with his hat, but as long as I was filling in the blanks in his sentences, it seemed— yes, prudent—to fill in some history, too.

"Yes," Joe said sweetly, his smile restored. "He was a good hunter."

This was going well, I thought—as well as any blind date with a man of few words. Thanks to Pransky, my natural reticence had melted away and had been replaced by a strange and unexpected gregariousness. Joe might be missing half his body, Pransky might be behaving crassly, I might be uncomfortable and out of my depth, but none of that seemed to matter much. Life was good. I had my hand on Pransky's back and Joe had his hand on her head and the three of us were getting serious hits of oxytocin—also known as the love hormone—as a consequence. In a 1999 study reported in the journal *Psychiatry*, researchers from the University of California–San Francisco found that elevated levels of oxytocin correlated with better interpersonal relationships. Check. Later studies, from Sweden and Japan, showed how oxytocin levels went up not only by petting a dog but by gazing at one as well, and as oxytocin increased, anxiety levels fell. Check. And we weren't the only ones love-drunk here. As random members of the staff passed down the hall and caught sight of the dog, they would tack in our direction, sail over, and touch Pransky as if she were a talisman.

"I need therapy, too," one of the nurses said. Though she might have been one of the housekeepers, or a medical technician, or a physical therapist, or from the kitchen staff. I couldn't tell the difference, and neither could Pransky, and the point was, it didn't matter.

"Hey, you're here," Janie said, coming up behind us. "I see you've met Joe. And don't you look adorable today!" she said, not to me. And Pransky did look adorable. She was wearing her crisp new red therapy dog bandanna and a yellow dog tag that declared "I am a therapy dog" with a phone number on the back in case something unfortunate were to happen. Week after week, this would be her uniform. "Time to get dressed for work!" I'd say, and she'd come trotting over and I'd slip off her worn purple everyday collar and snap on the brilliant red collar from which her official County Nursing Home and Rehabilitation Center picture ID, her TDI picture ID, and the yellow "I am a therapy dog" tag all hung. Then I'd tie the bandanna around her neck, smooth it out, and the transformation would be complete. Was it my imagination or, once she was dressed for work, did she stand taller, sit straighter, and look, well, expert?

As Janie walked with us down the hall, past the rooms of people who would be in the nursing home only for short stays while their knee replacements healed or pneumonia waned, I wanted to ask her about Joe or, more specifically, about Joe's legs. Diabetes seemed the most likely explanation, and I was curious and wanted to know if I was right. But there was no subtle way to ask, and there wasn't a good reason for me to know, so with Janie's confidentiality warning in mind, I didn't ask then, and I never asked later—not about Joe, not about anyone. I'd visit people, I'd talk to them month after month, and I might not know if they had some kind of cancer or had had a stroke or if their general decline was just a product of getting older. Sometimes they'd tell me. They'd say, "You know, I'm one year and eight months shy of one hundred, so I don't remember so well," or, "My niece brought me back from Florida after my husband died and I had this stroke," or, "The doctor says I have liver disease, not liver cancer." But for the most part I was in the dark about why they had ended up in County, and it took a while for me to be okay with that. Years before, I'd worked in and around prisons, where it was never okay to ask someone why they were incarcerated. It was simpler that way. Even so, the mind makes up stories according to familiar templates, so the young man I was interviewing one day, who was my age exactly, who had gone to prison the same year I'd gone to college, who said he missed riding his bike through the Pennsylvania countryside, who sometimes turned on the faucet in his cell and closed his eyes and imagined he was lying beside a rushing stream—he, I was certain, had done something stupid and impulsive and teenaged, like steal a car. And believing he'd done something stupid and impulsive like steal a car made it easier to talk to him and relate to him and feel for him, cooped up in a place corralled by razor wire. It didn't occur to me that you didn't get locked up in a place corralled by razor wire for stealing a car—not until he mentioned his friend, the one he'd fought with and killed. I'd liked my story better.

We rounded the corner and Janie sent us in to visit a woman named Lila Green with the words, "She loves dogs." The sentiment would have been obvious even without the introduction. Lila's bed was covered by a blanket with the image of a larger-than-life collie woven into it, there was a collie dog stuffed animal on her pillow, and pictures of collies torn from magazines were taped to her cupboard next to snapshots of babies and children in soccer and Little League uniforms.

"Come in, come in," she welcomed us. "Have a seat." Lila, in a pink velour jogging suit and fluffy pink slippers, was a robust woman with a cumulus cloud of hair topping a worn, rosy-cheeked face. She was sitting in an overstuffed easy chair, the only chair in the room, so I perched on the edge of the footboard, even as I vaguely remembered a rule about not sitting on a resident's bed. Was it because of the germs on the bed, I wondered, or the germs I'd be leaving on the bed, or was it because this was a resident's home, and that position was overly familiar?

"Sit, sit," Lila said. Pransky sat.

"What a good dog," Lila said. "I had a dog once."

had a dog once." Those were words I'd hear again and again. As soon as people saw Pransky, or put their hand in her hair and stroked her neck, they were transported back to some time and place in their life that was

not here or now. And it was odd—most of them had photos of children and grandchildren and great-grandchildren
tacked on the wall, not one or two, but lots of them, and
often, when I'd say, "Is this your granddaughter?" or,
"Who is in this photo?" they'd struggle, not just with the
name but with the nature of the relationship. It was different with their dogs. Ask the name of a pet from 1948
and the answer would bubble up as if it had been on the
surface all along, and with it came all sorts of stories and
details that were a testament to the deep connection at
work. "I had a dog once," a woman named Clara told me
more than once when Pransky and I passed her scuttling
along the hall in her wheelchair. "A poodle," she'd say.
"He was a beautiful dog. That's why they stole him."

"Who stole him?" I asked the first time.

"Magicians. Magicians came to my house and took
him when I wasn't looking." Her voice had dropped to a
conspiratorial whisper.

"When did this happen?" I asked.

"What kind of dog is he?" she responded, eyeing
Pransky.

Telling her that Pransky was part poodle seemed like
a very poor idea. "She's a mutt," I said evasively. "Also,

she's a she," I added, just in case there might be any (more) confusion here.

"My dog was beautiful," she said. "He was worth a lot of money. That's why they stole him."

"Sorry to hear that," I said, pulling on Pransky's leash and moving away from Clara. It was an interesting fantasy, and every time I'd see her, she'd tell me again, though with different particulars: sometimes the dog was a poodle, sometimes a German shepherd; sometimes it had been taken from her home by magicians, sometimes from the nursing home by robbers. The one consistent detail was that there had been a dog and it was gone, which could have been a metaphor, or could have been true, and in either case, Clara's sense of loss was palpable and real, which didn't make her seem any less nutty or Pransky any less eager to visit with her, or me any less likely to think my dog was nicer, had a bigger heart, was more tolerant, and was simply a better person than I was.

In *The Expression of the Emotions in Man and Animals*, which was published thirteen years after *On the Origin of Species*, Charles Darwin suggested that behaviors and attributes that we like to think of as exclusively human are more likely to have been handed down from our animal ancestors, so saying that my dog was a better person than I was made a certain amount of biological sense. Animals, Marc Bekoff and Jessica Pierce observed in their book *Wild Justice: The Moral Lives of Animals*, were often altruistic; showed compassion, empathy, and trust; and had "morality."

My empathetic dog, I was certain, knew right from wrong, which is the basis of a moral life. This was proved to me one afternoon when I left her in the car while I ran an errand.

"See you in a bit," I said to Pranny as I took a package of warm, aromatic, recently-retrieved-from-the-oven oatmeal fudge bars out of a plastic sack that I'd placed on the passenger-side floor and was delivering to a friend. It was the holiday season and I'd been handing these out all afternoon. After this delivery there was only one more to be made. Of course I wasn't worried about leaving my dog in the car with the cookies. I'd done it countless times before. We had an understanding, she and I. We followed the rules. She trusted me. I trusted her.

And there she was, ten minutes later, sitting in the backseat where I'd left her. I said hello and absently reached over and gave her head a pat as I slid back into the driver's seat. Just as I turned on the car, I heard a faint, unidentifiable sound, a rustling or possibly scratching. At the time, it meant nothing to me. I switched on the radio and drove.

The next part of the story is obvious, right? When I got to my destination and reached for the last package of oatmeal fudge bars, they were gone. And so was the aluminum foil in which they'd been wrapped, and so was the plastic bag in which they'd come. All of it was gone, without a trace. I turned and faced my dog. She was sitting up straight, looking past me. She seemed to be avoiding making eye contact. Eating all that chocolate was bad enough, but ingesting plastic and aluminum, too? That could not be good. While I was thinking this and the fatalistic, nightmarish cascade of thoughts that came with it, I heard that rustling-scratching sound again. It was as if a mouse was in the car. It wasn't so far-fetched—I'd once had a mouse family nesting in my gearbox. I looked down, prepared to see a small furry creature dragging its distended stomach across the upholstery. What I saw, instead, was my dog trying surreptitiously to move the only visible bit of evidence linking her to the crime, a small piece of the plastic bag, underneath her rear end, to get it out of sight.

"Stand up!" I commanded. Pransky pretended not to

hear. She was still looking out the window. She still had not looked at me. "Pransky," I said more sternly, "stand up!" She stayed seated. "Okay," I said, "you asked for it." I was about to deploy my weapon of last resort.

"Pransky," I said, "don't be a *bad dog*."

"Bad dog." She hated those words. I don't know how it happened, or when, but sometime early in her seven years, Pransky had internalized them. When she heard them, which was not more than a few times a year, she'd stop what she was doing, lower her head and tail, and look, well, ashamed. This may have been an anthropomorphic interpretation, but something resembling a conscience seemed to be at work. Those two words had power. They could make Pransky stop in her tracks. And the thing was, giving her the option not to be a bad dog was a direct challenge. It told her where she was heading, not where she was. "Don't be a bad dog!" Those words gave her the chance to do the right thing. And there was never a time when she didn't take it.

Pransky stood up. There was the bag and there was the aluminum foil. As for the cookies, every last crumb had disappeared. Pransky looked stricken. Was it her conscience, or was it her tummy? I did a quick calculation: she'd probably just swallowed a quarter-pound of chocolate, and since even small amounts of chocolate cannot be metabolized by a dog's body, she'd soon be in liver failure. Torn between holding my dog accountable for her theft and holding her close and comforting her during what were likely her last minutes on earth, I did neither. Instead, I called the vet.

"My dog just ate a lot of chocolate," I said when the receptionist picked up. "It was my fault," I added. "I left it in the car with her."

"Can I put you on hold?" she asked.

"No!" I said frantically. "My dog just ate chocolate."

"Dark chocolate or milk chocolate?" she inquired.

What? Was she joking? Did she think my dog was some kind of gourmand?

"Milk," I said.

"Good. I'm going to put you on hold." Minutes later, when she came back on the line after possibly dealing with someone whose dog had eaten one of those fancy, heart-healthy, fair trade, 90 percent cocoa super-dark chocolate bars that were sold at the local food co-op for $5 each, she explained that it was only pure chocolate that felled dogs. My dog, she said, would only feel bad.

"She already does," I said.

That, at least, was how it seemed to me, though it might not have looked that way to Bekoff and Pierce. Animal morality, they argued, was species specific. Rats had a rat-based moral code, for instance, and baboons had a baboon-based moral code, and they were not the same thing. Even within a species, Bekoff and Pierce pointed out, there could be variations in how norms of behavior were understood and expressed, so that what counted as "right" in one wolf pack might not be considered right in another. Yet while evolutionary biologists were able to point out examples of altruism, courage, justice, and cooperation in the animal kingdom, and while they could even codify the social norms of elephants, chimps, penguins, wolves, and bats, among others, it was different with dogs. Dogs live with us, and that changes everything.

The rules of engagement when dogs are together are not the same as when the pack is a mix of dogs and people. We teach our dogs right from wrong according to our understanding of right and wrong and what we want from them—no biting, no jumping, no stealing, no sticking their noses where they should not be—and most of the time, encouraged by occasional bits of beef jerky and peanut-butter dog biscuits, they abide. Whether their understanding of right and wrong is innate or learned, whether doing the right thing is self-motivated or driven by self-preservation, were interesting questions that were likely to be debated for a long time and possibly forever.

In the meantime, I understood something about practical wisdom and moral behavior that I hadn't before Pransky and I stepped into the nursing home: though I was in control of the leash, my dog was going to be my guide here. This was not because she was, as we like to imagine dogs, "nonjudgmental." I had to assume she was making judgments about people and situations all the time. But watching Pransky was a revelation. "Prudence is prescriptive," Aristotle wrote, "for its goal is determining what one must do or not do." What Pransky could do, and I could not, yet, was meet people exactly where they were (disabled, jolly, mute, demented, frail, lonely, tired, chatty), without a moment's hesitation, and that was a gift.

had a dog once," Lila said. "It lived for nine years and then it got heartworm, so we gave it arsenic to kill the worms, but the arsenic killed her."

So here was another small dilemma: someone you don't know tells you something intriguing but sad. Do you plumb the depths, or do you let it go? I decided to let it go.

"Let me guess," I said, teasing her a little. "Was your dog a collie?"

"Oh, yes," she said. "How did you know?"

Was Lila teasing back? Her rheumy eyes were unreadable, her smile nearly generic. It suddenly occurred to me that irony might have little place in the lives of the elderly. There was no time for it. And it could be confusing. Best to be as straightforward and direct as possible, I decided. Anything else was just cruel. Unless you were a dog.

While Lila and I were talking, Pransky stood up and slipped under Lila's tray table and approached Lila to be petted. When she did, Lila reached out and pushed the table, which was on wheels, to get better access to the dog. As she did, Pransky, tail wagging wildly, instantly backed away. It was like Doctor Dolittle's Pushmi-pullyu—as Pransky approached and Lila reached out, Pransky would retreat. This delighted Lila so much that she shut off *The Price Is Right*, which had been running in the background. Back and forth they went, like a band-

saw, which seemed pretty funny until I noticed that
Pransky's leash was caught in one of the table's wheels.
Every time Lila pushed the table away, Pransky had gone
with it. She hadn't been teasing, after all.

"Can you flip the TV back on, dear?" Lila asked as I
stood up to go.

"Of course," I said, and I did, and stayed for a few
minutes to watch the four contestants guess how much a
ten-megapixel single-lens reflex camera cost.

"How much do you think?" I asked Lila.

"Oh, I wouldn't know, dear," she said pleasantly, and
it occurred to me that she probably didn't care. Watching these screaming, hyperactive people and looking at
the shiny objects that were exciting them was like taking
a trip to another country. Maybe the television, which
was a constant presence in residents' rooms, was a kind
of babysitter, maybe it encouraged passivity, maybe it
was bad, but watching Lila watch it, I thought not. She
seemed genuinely fascinated by what she was seeing.
True, she could have been down in the activities room
for the Tuesday-morning sing-along, but who wanted to
revisit "Down by the Old Mill Stream," when an all-
expenses-paid, seven-day trip to Honolulu was in the offing? Lila was fully engaged. As she bid us to "come back

again next week," she did not turn from the screen, and I was, strangely, happy for her.

Lila's room was at the top of County's west wing, a location that meant little to me then, but was significant to the staff and some of the residents. The west wing was where people who had no serious memory problems were placed. These folks were, for the most part, cognitively intact—at least in comparison with the residents on the east side, many of whom wore ankle monitors to track their wanderings. While the west wing was where the chronically sick tended to stay—the people with breathing problems or heart problems or problems walking—it was also where the healthiest residents landed when they first arrived and where they might stay for a very long time. Clyde, whose room was at the opposite end of the hall from Lila's, had been a west wing resident for a dozen years—long enough to have had an affair with an aide, or so he liked to say, and to have scored the rare single room, which he decorated with medals and commendations from his Army service in World War II. Sitting in his wheelchair in his doorway, which at County was akin to sitting on your front porch, he could look across the hallway and through the window in his neighbor Shirley's room—she'd been here six years, though when I asked her how long she'd been at County she told me it had been three weeks—and get a good view of the raised beds where he grew Big Boy tomatoes and bush beans in the courtyard garden. Even in his eighties, with Coke-bottle spectacles, loose dentures, and a shrinking frame, Clyde was a big flirt. No woman, no matter what her age, could go by without him checking her out. "Bring the dog in closer," he'd say when Pranny and I would stop by, and of course I would, even after I realized it was a ploy so he could try to look down my shirt.

"He's playing us, Pran," I'd say sometimes after we'd left Clyde's room, and she'd wag her tail enthusiastically. "Play" was one of her words.

f we ever end up here ourselves, we are going to be the biggest pains-in-the-you-know-what," Janie and her assistant, Carol, joked one day when I asked why some residents got to live alone while others were doubled up with a roommate. Either they paid for the privilege,

Carol told me, or they were so ornery or demanding or obnoxious that no one could live with them. She didn't say which category Clyde fell into, and she didn't have to, since almost everyone's bill was paid for by some combination of Social Security, insurance, Medicaid, and Medicare. Clyde had been at County so long he had beaten the system.

Clyde's room and Lila's room and all the rooms, whether they were shared or not, were the same: square, with a big picture window looking out on a field or garden view, a closet and cupboard set, a nightstand, a rolling utility table that could slide up and over a bed, the bed, a chair, a bathroom. To these the residents added armchairs, flat-screen TVs, bookshelves, artwork, family photos, Red Sox and Patriots pennants, posters of muscle cars, and handmade quilts, so that their quarters more resembled the distinctive dorm rooms of the college down the road than the sterile wards of the hospital across the street. Like in a dorm room, the beds were typically side by side, so that people who had not known each other before might end up sleeping not more than a few feet apart, for years on end. Still, for a facility that relied on government money, County was pretty

nice. Though boxy and institutional, it was also comfortable and cheery, its muted yellow-and-blue hallways so
often bedecked by residents' handiwork and seasonal
decorations—flags on July Fourth, tinsel garlands and
candy canes at Christmas—that it sometimes resembled
an elementary school. And it was clean. This I knew for
sure because Pransky, who was always on the lookout for
anything of edible interest, rarely caused me to invoke
the censorious "leave it!" command as we strolled along
the hall. Sometimes, when we wandered into the dayroom, where some of the residents went after breakfast
to watch television or play cards, she'd find a stray scram-
ble of egg that had tumbled from someone's lap and
scarf it up before I could speak, but for the most part,
the furniture and floors of County were a food desert
for dogs.

On the other hand, for a dog like mine, with an
unhealthy affection for stuffed animals, County was
a dream. Almost everyone had at least one plush toy
on their bed, and some rooms looked like the stuffed
animal department at a Toys"R"Us superstore because,
in addition to being proxies for love and affection,
stuffed animals were sometimes handed out as prizes

at Friday-afternoon bingo games. It was either stuffed animals or quarters, and since the animals' currency was denominated in tenderness, and there was little opportunity to spend money, quarters had less value.

When she first dropped us off at Lila's room, Janie had given me a list with the names and room numbers of residents who wanted a visit from Pransky, and it seemed that almost everyone did. We made our way down the west corridor, and I would knock on each door, even if it was open; say, "Dog visit"; and enter. By the third room, my assumption that the residents of County spent their days languishing in bed had been excised; everyone was showered, fed, and dressed for the day, even those who found this all so exhausting they were nodding off again. Like Fran. That first day, when Pranny and I stepped into her room she was on her back, eyes closed, lying in a bed covered with books and mail, propped up by a gang of pillows, wearing a washed-out 2004 Red Sox World Series sweatshirt and a pair of matching sweatpants, her breathing assisted by a green oxygen tank parked in the corner. "Dog visit," I said, and she perked right up and invited us in, in a warm, smoky voice. Fran's skin was the color of her clothes, but her eyes were keen and intelligent, like my dog's.

"Tell me about her," she said before we had made it across to her side of the room, the far side, which looked out onto a flat expanse of grass and trees that were just beginning to turn. So I did. I told her about Pransky's name, and how she got it, and how we got her, and how I trained her, and about the test, because every time I was about to stop talking and ask Fran a question, she jumped the queue and put another question to me. It was very skillful, and pretty soon she was asking me about my family, our house, our town, the books I was reading. When I finally got a question in, it was no longer about dogs or the weather or the pictures on her wall. It was "Were you a reporter?"

Most of the time when we see an old person, or a sick person, what we "get" is what we see: someone who is old, or someone who is sick, as if each of these things were an identity. I'd once spent a week observing the goings-on in the intensive care unit of a major New York City hospital, where the people in the beds were treated, essentially, as an algebraic equation, with variables for respiration, heart rate, oxygenation, fluid retention, consciousness. To the people monitoring and fiddling with the equation, nothing but the numbers mattered. History didn't matter. Context didn't matter. What the philosophers call personhood didn't matter. So it was a shock when family and friends assembled, or when an obituary appeared in the newspaper, to find out that these had been people, and they had had lives—rich, rewarding, interesting, challenging, complicated lives. They had been parents and children, they had gone to school, they had gone to war, they knew things no one else did, they had partners and spouses, they built things, they read books, they wrote books.

It was the same in the nursing home. Everyone arrived with a past, but it was like a coat you checked at the door. So you once ran a school. So you were a radiologist, or a car mechanic. So you were a line cook in El Paso—you wouldn't be cooking again. So you were a nurse—now you were attended by nursing assistants. In studies, people say that what they fear most about moving into a place like County is losing their independence. They are afraid, in other words, of ceasing to be what they were. Autonomy is imbued with history. When the bell tolls for the one, it also tolls for the other.

The reporter question was right on target. Fran had worked for a small newspaper in Virginia, where she went after graduating from college in Vermont. But newspapering wasn't satisfying, and after a few years Fran moved back north, did public relations for universities and hospitals, and then switched gears and became a drug and alcohol counselor. She didn't say why. Like many people who are good at asking questions, Fran was not so great with the answers. When she wanted to change the subject, she brought the conversation back to the dog.

"I had a colleague once whose name was Pransky," she said. "Any relation?" It was clear from her tone that she hadn't thought much of this Pransky. Did I admit he was a distant relative I'd never met? Would that Pransky taint this Pransky?

Hearing her name, Pransky migrated from the floor at the end of Fran's bed to a place closer to her face, but given the height of the bed, Fran's arthritic hands, and Pransky's smallish stature, they couldn't connect. There was a chair in the corner and I moved it next to the bed and invited Pranny to climb into it, which she did. Janie happened to walk by right then and did a double take: Pransky looked like a doctor consulting with her patient, which in a way she was. But pretty soon she had slid her front paws into the bed, and then rearranged herself so that only her hindquarters were in the chair while the rest of her was on the mattress, with her right paw on top of Fran's right hand. Suddenly, out of nowhere, Fran's roommate began to moan.

"Should I do something?" I asked Fran, who did her best to roll her eyes. One eye was having muscle trouble, and a trip to the ophthalmologist was on her schedule.

"She does this all the time," she said without a speck of concern. "Tell me about the class you're teaching at the college."

I heard myself talking, but even more, I heard the woman in the next bed whimpering loudly. Pransky was unconcerned, which seemed significant. In bad storms, or when the coyotes bayed in the woods around our house at night, I often looked to see if she was rattled, and if she was not, I figured there was no reason to be worried. Still, I wondered if Fran's lack of concern was the equivalent of walking past a homeless person panhandling on the street. We all did it. I got that. But wasn't the point of the parable of the Good Samaritan not only that he stopped to help the man who was ailing on the side of the road, but that no one else did? I wanted to do the right thing here, but I didn't know what that was. Should I defer to the person in the room with the most experience, or should I be concerned that her experience had made her insensitive? It was the same old dilemma: If I didn't know, how could I know? "Most people do not perform virtuous actions, they take refuge in reasoning about them and they imagine they are doing philosophy and becoming good in this way," Aristotle wrote. I wasn't imagining that I was doing philosophy. I was imagining I was doing nothing while this poor woman shucked her mortal coil.

I pressed the call button.

This time Fran succeeded in rolling both eyes.

"Sorry," I said. "I'm a rookie."

"What is going on with the Red Sox?" she asked. It was an interesting segue.

"I read this morning that the Red Sox are thinking of trading Mike Lowell," I said to her, my words underscored by a particularly long and loud moan from the next bed.

"What a shame," Fran said. "He's so cute."

Before too long, an unsmiling aide appeared.

"What's the problem?" she asked.

"She sounds bad," I said, pointing to the roommate, who was lying on top of her covers in a fetal position, eyes wide open. It was freaky, but only, I guess, to me.

"She's fine," the aide said, all business, "but your dog's paw is blocking Fran's air supply."

I looked down and, sure enough, Pransky's left paw was resting on about an inch of the long plastic conduit running between the oxygen tank in the corner of the room and the nasal cannula that wrapped around Fran's face.

"It's their first day," Fran said to the aide, who just nodded and told her that she would be back in a minute with her medicine. I didn't know what kind of medicine that was, but it felt too personal to stick around to find out, so I said our goodbyes.

"Make sure you come back next week," Fran said. "Wake me if you have to. This was fun."

"We will. And we'll try not to kill you," I said. "It was fun."

Fun" is not a word I would have associated with spending time in a nursing home before Pranny and I found ourselves spending time in a nursing home.

Depressing, maybe, or unpleasant or sad, but not fun or enjoyable or entertaining. When friends heard that Pransky and I were spending a couple of hours a week together at County they invariably said it was good of us to be doing that. I might have said the same thing to a friend of mine, and the good to which I would have been referring was the trade-off between doing something, seemingly, for others, instead of something more obviously self-interested, like sleeping in or going skiing or reading a novel. It took a few visits to understand that even if Pranny and I were doing good by being there, being there was not a trade-off with anything. Hanging out at County with my dog turned out to be as satisfying as anything else we could have been doing between ten and noon on Tuesdays, and, most of the time, more so.

To the economists and neuroscientists who study in the newly minted field of neuroeconomics, this revelation of mine would not have been surprising. A group at the University of Oregon, for instance, used functional magnetic resonance imaging (fMRI) to "see" people's motives for making charitable donations. What they found was that for some people—about half in their experiment—giving away money made them as happy as being given free money. Everyone liked getting money, but for some, charity triggered the same pleasure response in the brain. So, on the theory that time is money, it's no wonder why spending it at County was fun: my ventral striatum was glowing.

In this case, it might seem that no one was handing me money, but consider this: in a 2010 study on the health benefits of volunteering, 73 percent of the respondents said that volunteering lowered their stress levels, 89 percent said it improved their sense of well-being, and 92 percent reported that it enriched their sense of purpose in life. These results reaffirmed the work done by researchers from the University of Wisconsin–Madison, who looked at data from the Wisconsin Longitudinal Study, which has followed more than ten thousand men and women since they graduated from high school in 1957. In their work, they found a causal relationship between doing good and feeling good. Add this to the finding of researchers at the universities of Michigan, Rochester, and Stony Brook, which showed that people who volunteered lived, on average, four years longer than those who did not, and the word "fun" begins to make a lot more sense. To put into scientific terms what was happening when Pransky and I were welcomed into a resident's room or stopped in the hallway so someone could talk to the dog: we were winning a lottery we hadn't known we were playing.

P ransky and I continued down the hall. In the day-room we encountered a grizzled old guy in front of the TV, who didn't look away from the screen when we approached, but reached out and silently summoned the dog. She stood there, blissfully arching her neck as he massaged her back between the shoulders. He never spoke, but someone else told me his name was Thomas and that he'd run a modest family farm two towns over, in a small agricultural hollow that was now known for its artisanal cheeses. Lizzie was sitting in the same room as Thomas, planted in a Barcalounger, her eyes trained on the same screen, her head listing to one side. She was young, maybe thirty-five, maybe forty-five, with long brown hair, soft eyes, and fingers that tapered like a pia-nist's. They were painted baby-doll pink, which seemed appropriate: there was something delicate and fragile about her.

"Hi, Lizzie," I said. "Do you want to say hi to the dog?"

Her eyes lit up, but she, too, said nothing. I pushed

Pransky forward, since she didn't seem inclined to move there on her own; the big chair, with its leg rest extending upward, was intimidating.

"Would you like to pet her?" I asked, though I had no idea whether Lizzie understood me or not. I was thinking stroke and cerebral palsy and car accident. I was thinking of every bad thing that could have happened to land her at County, knowing that one in seven nursing home residents was now under sixty-five, and the number was growing fast. People in their thirties and forties, whose lives had deviated from the standard for any number of unforeseen and unforgiving reasons, who could not be cared for at home, were landing among the elderly because there was no place else for them to get twenty-four-hour care, especially since the government, while willing to foot that bill, was typically unwilling to pay relatives to care for them at home, even when that was the cheaper alternative.

I continued to edge Pransky as close to Lizzie as she could get, and while I felt her body resisting, she let me do it anyway. Petting the back of her head, I steered and pushed till it was resting on Lizzie's thigh.

Lizzie extended her fingers—this seemed hard for her—and touched the dog. And smiled. "Puppy," she said.

"Puppy," I said. And in the context of that room, that one word felt like a conversation.

Still, if I was ever open to the notion that a therapy dog team doesn't really do anything therapeutic, it would have been that first morning at County, when everyone was a stranger, and Pransky and I dipped in and out of rooms, never quite sure of our bearings. We were like speed daters, or out-of-town visitors at a party; the point was to circulate and meet as many people as possible. Lizzie and Thomas, sitting mutely in their chairs, sunshine taking over the room like the most garrulous guest—what were we to them, I wondered. Intruders? Indistinguishable members of that phalanx of people who marched through their lives every day, dispensing this and that? Sorcerers, conjuring a different time and place as residents' fingers uncurled into Pransky's fur? Sorcery that someone else might call "therapy"? Watching Lizzie's eyes—which had been unfocused before they settled on Pranny—watching them register what they were seeing and then react ("Puppy!"), was not only like seeing a synapse lay down a bridge, connect axon to dendrite and proliferate wide and far, it was feeling the synapses fire in my own brain. Sometimes, and maybe more often than we realize, understanding—cognition—is a physical sensation. And what I was feeling was that my dog had the capacity for a deeper conversation in that place than I, with all the words in the dictionary at my disposal, would ever have. A dog goes from "hello" to "I could really love you" in an instant, and means it. If there was therapy happening, it was happening in the ellipsis that connected the one to the other.

Though not for everyone. "Get your goddamned dog out of here!" a man rolling down the hallway in his wheelchair hissed at us as we left the dayroom. He looked nice enough, a regular guy, in jeans, a faded green turtleneck, and boat shoes, no socks—so nice, in fact, that I thought he was kidding, and laughed.

"Nothing funny about it," he growled. "You heard me." He leaned back in his chair and, with the agility and mordant rage of an urban driver on a mission, aimed the wheels at Pranny and me so we had no choice but to scoot into the nearest room.

"Um, hi!" I said brightly to the occupants. One, whose back was to us, was reading the newspaper. The other, in the far corner of the room, looked up from her Nora Roberts novel with a degree of alarm. She was, despite the expression on her face, quite adorable, with white hair that sat upon her head in tight curls, a white cardigan with plastic mother-of-pearl buttons, a *Little House on the Prairie* long pink skirt, and bright white Velcro-fastened sneakers so clean they looked like they'd never touched the ground. She was the ur-great-grandmother among all the other great-grandmothers.

I looked down at the clipboard that held the "Pranny list" of people we were supposed to visit and pretended to consult it, but the truth was that we had jumped into the room so quickly I had no clue which it was. And not knowing which room it was meant I had no idea whose room it was, or if we were even supposed to be there.

"Would you like a visit from the dog?" I asked the room at large, but only the woman in the corner responded. She shook her head, no.

"I don't much like dogs," she said, and when she spoke, it was almost in a vibrato. Her words, which came out slowly, and in a breathy, high-pitched tone, seemed to shake. As we conversed, Pransky used the slack in her leash to get closer to the woman reading the newspaper, who noticed the dog when she turned the page and nearly flew out of her chair.

"Look who is here!" she exclaimed loudly, dropping the paper and pushing away her utility table so she could hug Pransky.

"She loves dogs so much I'm certain she is part dog," the adorable woman in the corner said in her slow, strange, tremulous voice.

"What's her name?" I asked, as if the other woman wasn't right there, playing happily with my dog.

"Dottie," she said. And then, after a long pause to catch her breath: "She's completely deaf. Can't hear a thing."

"Ohhh," I said.

Dottie. I checked my list. She must be Dottie Marsh, and this had to be room 143. I checked again.

"You're not on the list," I said to the woman who was not Dottie. "Do you really not like dogs?"

"I like some dogs," she said.

"You'll like my dog," I said. And I was right.

Her name was Iris. Iris and Dottie. One couldn't hear, which was fine, since the other had such a hard time talking. If a biology student needed an irrefutable illustration of symbiosis, it was these two. Years before they'd come to room 143 as strangers; over time they'd gotten close as sisters, and as that happened, the distance between their beds grew smaller and smaller till now it could be measured in inches.

"I don't know what I'd do without her," Iris told me

months later, days after Dottie had fallen in the bathroom, hit her head, and ended up with a bunch of stitches and a black eye. And the thing was, they never talked. They just knew. They knew the way Pransky knew.

"There's my dog," Dottie said more than a few times to Pransky, even though they'd just met. "That's a good fella!" She and Iris were beaming at Pranny and me. "You just made my week," Dottie said to us as we were leaving.

There was a Halloween aspect to walking the halls at County. Even armed with the list of people who, at their intake interview (which could have been years before), had indicated that they liked dogs, it was hit or miss at every doorway. I'd knock and ask if they'd like a visit from Pransky, which was a treat for most but a trick for some. Like Vinny. Vinny was famous. Everyone knew Vinny, who was the mascot and biggest booster of the local college football and basketball teams. A middle-aged man with a severe case of cerebral palsy, he'd ended up in County when his parents died earlier in the year, and he wasn't too happy about it. At home he'd been the center of attention. Here he was just one of the crowd.

At home there was a fair amount of stimulation. Here, not so much. Vinny spent most days cutting and pasting articles about his teams into a scrapbook, which was no small feat for someone with limited fine motor skills. Saturday afternoons in the fall, big, hulking wide receivers and tackles picked him up—literally—and carried him to the stadium. During basketball season, big, tall guys came and brought him to the gym. They had such a long tradition of getting him to their games that Vinny and his boys had been featured on ESPN and in the pages of *Sports Illustrated*.

"Hey, come here!" Vinny called out as Pranny and I were passing his room. I looked at the list. He was not on it, but his roommate, who was not in the room, was.

I stopped. "Us?" I asked.

"No," he said. "You. Not your dog. Dogs make me sneeze."

"You're Vinny," I said. "You're famous."

"Yes, I am," he said, in an uninflected, matter-of-fact way. "Come here. Don't bring the dog."

Did I dare? This was the real-world application of test number thirteen, the drop-the-leash-and-walk-away test. What if Pransky took off and slipped into someone's room, surprised them, and triggered a heart attack? Or tripped someone pushing a walker down the hall? Or sampled the medicine-laced applesauce at the nurses' station? I gave her a long look and crossed my arms. She slid to the floor, haunches folded under her torso, lying down, yes, but in the perfect position from which to launch herself up the hall.

"Stay," I said, dropping the leash and raising my palm like a traffic cop.

I walked backward into Vinny's room, keeping my eye on the dog the whole time.

"No dog," he said.

"No dog," I said, holding out my hands to prove I wasn't trying to pull a fast one. "She's really nice, though," I ventured.

"No dog," he said. So much for small talk. Vinny needed me to reach under his bed and pull up a file folder full of newspaper articles, which meant I had to turn my back on my partner. It occurred to me that the real test here was not of her but of me: Did I really trust her?

The relationship between the members of a therapy dog team is based on two complementary beliefs. The first is that the handler has to believe that the dog will know how to behave and what to do, which often means deferring to the handler, looking to her for guidance, and following through on her commands. The second is that the dog, for her part, has to believe that the handler has her best interests at heart. All morning, as we made our way around this unfamiliar place that was full of new and peculiar smells, with people reaching out to touch her and grab her tail and pull her ears, Pransky stayed on task, looking at me constantly for an expression, a gesture, a word that would let her know I knew what was happening and that it was all okay.

If I had been unaware that she was working hard and that paying such close attention was physically draining, Pransky let me know the second we entered Geri's room, at about the ninety-minute mark. Because Geri was blind and had balance issues, her bed was low to the ground, about seven inches from the floor, which was covered with blue tumbling mats just in case. When we walked in, Geri wasn't in bed but was sitting in a nearby chair, headphones on, listening to an audiobook. She could neither see nor hear us, which turned out to be fortuitous, because, without missing a step, Pransky walked onto Geri's bed and stretched out.

"Illegal, illegal," I whispered to her. "You know

better." But maybe she didn't. From her vantage point, it probably looked like that low bed had been put there for her benefit. Pransky stood up and got down, even though it was obvious that she was tired and needed to rest. Time may be universal, but none of us experiences it the same way. For Pransky, an hour and a half in the woods, racing around, following her own nose, was no time at all—it was minutes factored in dog years. For Pransky in the nursing home, listening to my words, reading my gestures, executing my commands, ninety minutes was something else entirely. It was dense and hard and unrelenting. I slipped the headphones from Geri's ears and asked her if she'd like to pet my dog. Pransky yawned and stepped forward.

"At your service," she seemed to be saying.

am not sure how long it takes to achieve practical wisdom. Aristotle, for one, is intentionally fuzzy, and, anyhow, I was under no illusion that I'd be much wiser at the end of the morning than I was at the beginning, though I actually think I was. I knew more about my dog, and what she could teach me, and more about myself, and what I needed to learn. At first it seemed that achieving practical wisdom would be like climbing to the top of a tall mountain and finally being able to see the panorama as it could never have been seen from below. But that didn't account for whatever vistas were gained on the way up. And then it dawned on me that I was focused on the climber when I should have been looking at the mountain. Mountains form by accretion, by opposing forces pushing up against each other. Aristotle says that prudence is not available to the young and it turns out that this is why: it develops slowly, in geologic time, imperceptibly, but constantly.

That first morning I got Vinny his folder, set it on the bed beside him, helped him with a few scrapbooking tasks, and then made my exit. Pransky was waiting right where I'd left her, on the hallway floor, checking out the action but staying out of it.

"Sorry I doubted you," I said. "Doubt" was not one of her words.

3.

Faith

Faith, which is often considered to be the opposite of doubt, was not one of my words. Its meaning was nebulous, obscure, debatable, personal. The dictionary said faith was "the complete trust or confidence in someone or something." That was the first meaning, and in the context of what Pransky and I were doing together at County on Tuesday mornings, it was clear that faith had to precede trust. To do this work right, not only did I have to trust my dog, as I've said, but I also had to have faith in her. Faith was the paradoxical element that fueled everything we did there—think of it as hydrogen, sitting at the top-left corner of the periodic table, at once the most universally abundant and the rarest element on earth. This is what I was learning and what she was teaching. People joke that "dog" is "God" spelled backward, which may be because the animal relationship is the clearest manifestation of the ineffable many of us get. When the Swiss psychiatrist Carl Jung was asked about his belief in God, he famously said that he didn't "believe," he "knew." That was faith, and whether Pransky was spelled forward or backward, my faith was aspirational, though less so as we spent more time together, and I became a better student of hers. Her behavior wasn't perfect. She sometimes still pulled on her leash, and sometimes, mesmerized by the mob of pigeons that congregated at the bird feeders placed strategically outside each resident's window, she'd ignore the person we'd come to visit. But who among us is perfect? Perfection is too high a bar, and it may be what separates the gods from the rest of us.

In college I'd read the Protestant theologian Paul Tillich's definition of faith, that it is "the state of being ultimately concerned," which he followed up by saying that "the ultimate is concerned about what is experienced as ultimate." Reading those words again brought to mind Pransky chasing her tail. Still, sometimes, if only for a few seconds, she actually caught it. (Was that transcendence?)

"An act of faith is an act of a finite being who is grasped by and turned to the infinite," I also read in Tillich, searching as I think I was for guidance about those "finite beings" Pransky and I were spending time with at County, and how their experience might foretell mine. Unlike restraint and prudence (and justice and courage), which are considered cardinal virtues and speak to our character, faith, along with love and hope, is a theological virtue, said to emanate from God. The question on my (secular, Jewish-married-to-a-Methodist-Sunday-school-teacher) mind was: Did God or religion or faith—whatever that was—become more present and more important when you lived—not to put too fine a point on it—in the shadow of death? While it's true that we all live in that shadow, at the nursing home it was darker, wider, longer, and, plainly, more obvious.

don't know what I believe anymore," Barbara Burch told me one morning when Pransky and I stopped by to see her on the east wing. "It's very confusing, and it gets more confusing all the time." She was ninety-one then, and had lived a comfortable life, as the wife of a civil engineer and the mother of three children.

I would have thought that the older you got, the more secure you were in your beliefs, I told her, though I knew as soon as I said it that the opposite could have been just as true. This assumption—that the nearer you are to death, the more appealing the consolations of religion—was based on nothing, really, except deathbed scenes from movies and stories of death-row inmates who got religion before their executions. Was I somehow, unconsciously, thinking that the people at County had been condemned to die? It was an interesting question. Unless they got transferred to the hospital, they would all die there, yes (except for the ones on the rehabilitation wing), but its likely location was the only thing they knew about their death that the rest of us didn't. Even that much knowledge, though, made death seem real and imminent in a way that it doesn't, otherwise. We're all condemned to die, but so what? If you spent a lot of time worrying about the details, you'd never get out of bed in the morning. (And you'd never be able to sleep.) Barbara, though, looked the picture of health. Her blue eyes were lucid and clear, she made it a point to walk outside most days, and she was involved in two ongoing bridge games.

"I know I don't believe in hell," she said after a while. "That is one thing I believe. I'm just not sure about heaven. All I can do is trust Jesus."

I didn't get a chance to ask what that meant since the lunch cart was arriving, but I'm not sure Barbara would have been able to answer, anyhow. After a certain point, asking for rational answers to feelings, or passions, or "knowing not believing" is beside the point. At ninety-one, the scaffolding might have broken down some, but Barbara still had something essential to hang on to, and it was good. It only occurred to me later that her doubt was as clear an expression of faith as there could be. The false certainties (hell) had worn away with time, and there might not be an eternal reward (heaven), but even so, and in spite of this, she surrendered her trust to Jesus.

"People go out the way they came in," the medical director at County told me when I asked if she'd noticed people moving toward religion or faith or God or anything spiritual at the end of their days. What she meant, she said, was that in her experience, people didn't automatically become more reflective as they grew old, and they did not suddenly become seekers if they had never been. The habit of religion stays there if it's there, she said, but it's a rare person who develops it late in life.

I hadn't been looking for exceptions the day Pranny and I encountered Ani on the rehab wing, sitting in her room, fingering a beaded bracelet as if it were a rosary, meditating before a small altar she'd assembled on her windowsill. She was old the way the wind is old, old beyond time, her hair shaved to white stubble, her blue eyes sunken behind round, wire-framed glasses, her fingers bony, her arms bony, her shoulders rising up like goal posts under her maroon sweatshirt and maroon down vest. In Buddhism, the name Ani is used to address a woman in monastic clothes whose status is unknown. In Ani's case it was because, despite her advanced age, she was a novitiate who until she came to County had been living in a Buddhist nunnery, working her way up the spiritual ladder—though I don't think she would have described it precisely like that. Ani was a relatively new name. For nearly seventy years she'd had another one, a more conventional name, just like she'd had a more conventional life, working in the printing trade in New York City and raising her two sons. Buddhism appealed to her; she started a practice. But it was only after she'd retired that she embraced it wholly, divesting herself of her old life and taking on a new one, with a new identity as a Buddhist nun who gave up her city apartment for an ascetic's cell in Vermont. Ani lived in community. She prayed. She was silent. And she was, she told me, happy and sustained by this. "I am full," she said, as if we'd been talking about food instead of about letting go. It was pretty clear that she was dying—she had cancer and needed oxygen to breathe. But it was equally clear that she was full of life, still curious, and still reaching out with what seemed to be youthful vigor.

"There's a dog at the monastery now," she said in a breathy voice. "The abbess had never had a dog, and then one night she had a dream that left her craving a dog, and then a dog basically dropped into her lap. She named the dog Emma, but no one knows how to train her, so she's become a lap dog." Ani wanted to know how I'd trained Pransky, so I told her about starting with verbs, then moving to nouns, making sure to maintain eye contact at all times. Then I showed her some basic hand commands—sit, come, lie down, stay—and she wanted to try them out on Pransky, who was game.

"This is fun!" she said as Pransky slid down on her haunches at the crossed-arms command, then rose to her feet when Ani gave the sign for "stand up." Then Ani stopped talking, and her gaze drew inward and it was as if she were gone. It was a brief departure, but an abrupt one, and then she was back. "Sorry," Ani said. "Sometimes I just lose track. What's the dog's name again? She is beautiful."

"How do we prepare for death?" I read on a Buddhist website a few weeks later, after I'd gone to start a fire in the woodstove and come across Ani's obituary in the newspaper I was crumpling up. "It is really simple, just behave in a manner which you believe is responsible, good and positive for yourself and towards others. This leads to calmness, happiness and an outlook which contributes to a calm and controlled mind at the time of death."

This was advice meant for the dying, but it worked for me, too. A purple name tag on a resident's room meant that the resident was in hospice care, and at first I avoided those rooms, telling myself that the last thing a dying person needed was a happy-go-lucky dog taking up their precious last earthly moments. (This turned out to be overly dramatic, since plenty of people in hospice care lived for months, and a few even recovered enough to get their old white name tags back.) Then one day a woman with a purple name tag called out to us as we walked by her room, beckoning us to come in. Maisie was bored and chatty, and invited Pransky to get in bed with her as she engaged me in a spirited discussion about the psychology of the former Red Sox slugger Manny Ramirez, who had just taken himself out of the game after testing positive for performance-enhancing drugs. Maisie thought Manny was "a good boy who had made bad choices" and even seemed willing to forgive him for becoming a Dodger. Talking with her, I forgot all about the purple sign outside her door—or, rather, I let go of my assumptions about the purple sign. Maisie might not have had long to live, but she wasn't dead yet and there was no reason to treat her like she was. ("Not knowing how close the truth is, we seek it far away," I read on another Buddhist website.)

In the photograph accompanying the obituary in the paper, a skeletal Ani was sitting on a chair in her maroon robes, a smile playing at the edges of her mouth, which was pursed, blowing soap bubbles. "She had a strong belief that life does not end when the physical body dies, but instead, begins yet another journey," it said.

So there I was, on a journey with my dog, on a path that was less straightforward than I'd imagined it would be. It started at home, which had become remarkably less homey with Sophie away at school, and where her words, spoken years before as an eight-year-old after our beloved golden retriever Barley had died—that our family didn't seem complete without a dog—now seemed fundamentally wrong. We had a dog: it was Sophie's absence that mattered. If, before she left, I lived in the messy thicket of motherhood, I now found myself in a clearing without obvious landmarks, wondering which way to go. It was disorienting, but it wasn't bad, and it wasn't bad because any way forward was possible, including the way that led me to people like Ani.

Before Pranny and I started spending Tuesdays at County, I held the standard assumptions about what it would be like there. (One article I read was titled "Are Nursing Homes Better Than Death?" which pretty much summed up my expectations and, most likely, yours.) While many of my negative assumptions were gone by the time we'd finished our first rounds that first day, a more deeply embedded notion persisted and took a while to go away. It was that old age was, essentially, the same as middle age, only a few years later. While that was true chronologically, chronology was only one dimension in a person's life. Many of the things most of us fear about nursing homes—that they spell a loss of independence, of autonomy, of privacy—have already been realized before a person takes up residence in one. People typically landed in County because old age was distinctly different from middle age—maybe they were no longer mobile, maybe their brain was fuzzy, maybe the demands of a chronic disease were too much to manage. Once that was acknowledged, there would be a cascade of other things to acknowledge, too, starting with the incontrovertible truth that the book of life always has a concluding chapter. Ani embraced this and died blowing bubbles.

For my part, after a few weeks, I had learned the residents' names, and where they were from, and what they had done in their lives. It was the rare person who hadn't grown up on a farm, or farmed for a living, or married a farmer, though there were teachers, artists, factory workers, college professors, truck drivers, doctors, homemakers, and store clerks among them. Old age and illness are the great levelers, so a Yale graduate who had been the headmaster of a New England boarding school could end up in a room with a man who left school at sixteen and spent much of his adult life riding a tractor, cutting and baling hay, and it might not be obvious to an outsider which was which. They got along all right, too, Scotty and Dan, at least in the beginning, before Scotty started bursting into song at high volume at inopportune times, and Dan threatened to get violent. But back when they were friendly, Dan asked me to take him to the activities room and show him pictures of Scotty's old school on the computer, which I was happy to do, because that was the school where Sophie was studying, and there was a chance that I'd catch a glimpse of her in one of the school's online photo albums.

It was early October and she was on "solo," a three-day wilderness expedition where each student was given food and water, a sleeping bag, a tarp, matches, and an alcohol stove and dropped off, alone, in the New Hampshire mountains, to confront herself and ponder creation and the cosmos—or, if not that, at least to make it through those long nights and days and emerge to tell the tale. Though it was a controlled experiment—the students had whistles and an emergency flagging system—and though Sophie was an accomplished hiker who had spent countless nights outdoors, I was worried. As her mother, it was my prerogative to worry. It was rainy and cold out, the perfect conditions for hypothermia, and the weather report mentioned the possibility of both light-ning and flurries in the range where I was pretty sure she had set up camp. I imagined the night sky crackling with electricity. I imagined the trees above her sizzling as they were struck. I imagined those flashes of light illuminating her fear and the rain pouring down and collecting on the ground and seeping under the tarp, soaking the sleeping bag, and her shivering for hours on end. She was far away and out of touch, so the helicopter parent in me was grounded. Looking at pictures from earlier in the semes-ter, when the tomatoes in the school garden were ripe on the vine and the students walked barefoot over the soft grass, was the perfect antidote to obsessing about the snow that was predicted to follow the rain in the higher elevations that first night.

So Scotty, Dan, and I huddled around the computer, and as I scrolled through the albums, Scotty showed Dan his old house, and the garden and animals that supplied most of the school's food, and the woodlot that heated it, and they could make out the hop hornbeam and Norway spruce, and they could agree on the beauty of tamaracks in winter when their shaggy coats yellowed and stood out against the leafless grays of the birch and beech trees. Because I'd recently been over to the school, I could tell them stories about the place, like the time I was walking the trail to the sugar house with Pransky, past a field with draft horses so tall and wide that from a distance they looked like outbuildings, and up past another field flocked with sheep, which were guarded by an imperious llama. The sheep were running about, which looked like good fun to Pransky, who slipped under the electric fence and started running with them. Frightened, they ran full tilt one way till they could go no farther, ran another way, and another, going quickly together, as if they'd been choreographed, with Pransky on their heels and me on the other side of the fence, yelling for her to come back. Too enthralled to listen, she kept this up for a while, until the llama, incensed at this breach of protocol, stomped over and looked like he was about to eat Pransky for lunch. Terrified, she scooted under the fence and kept going for another quarter-mile. By the time I caught up with her she was panting and covered in muck, and seemed to welcome the decisive snap of the leash as I attached it to her collar.

And I could tell Scotty things about the school that had happened since he'd last been there, like the French teacher's new baby, and the director's new wife. To each bit of news he'd respond, "You don't say!"—amazed, it seemed, by the ordinary progression of life. But then he'd point to an otherwise indistinguishable window: "That's the room where I taught math." And "I planted that lilac for my wife." It was clear that while his memory had been quickly and dramatically eroded by a cerebral hemorrhage a few months before and was unreliable, it still held on to the most salient facts.

"I met your wife," I said to him.

"You don't say!" he said.

"Yes," I said, and mentioned her name.

"That *was* her name!" he said, incredulous. It was like all of a sudden I was a messenger from a different corner of the universe.

"It was back when I was on the school's advisory board. With you," I said.

"You were on the advisory board with me?" he asked.

"Yes," I said. "Four years ago."

"You don't say!"

At the time, Scotty was still living near the school, tending mainly to his wife, who was in the later stages of dementia. I remember him coming to a board meeting dressed in his tan, wide-wale corduroys and plaid wool shirt, his white hair flowing, telling us how sad it was to watch his beloved slip away. He seemed fine then, hearty and articulate, his mind sharp and incisive. If you'd told me then that I'd be seeing him at County four years later, struggling to remember the simplest things, unable to follow the caller at bingo or the clues for a child's crossword puzzle, I would not have believed you. I didn't believe myself: I'd walked right by him for weeks. He was just another old guy nodding off in his wheelchair.

The brain relies on pattern recognition to see, and Scotty, who came not only from a different part of the state but from a place of intellectual engagement and sophistication, was not the sort of person who I assumed I'd find at County, especially not on the east wing. It was Janie's assistant, Carol, who mentioned in passing that one of the residents on the memory wing had founded the school where my daughter was studying. I simply hadn't seen him. I had seen only a name on the list of residents who had requested dog visits, and as Scotty was a nickname, it had triggered no recognition. I had seen a man who bungled the words to "How Great Thou Art" at the Methodist service, but who sang with such gusto that the words seemed irrelevant. I saw a man who greeted Pransky by name each week, which was impressive until I realized he was reading it off the whiteboard in the hall that announced the day's activities. "Pransky Dog Visits," it said, and when Scotty saw the dog he'd consult the whiteboard and call her over. If at first I was impressed that he remembered her name, later I was impressed that he still remembered how to read.

Sophie didn't freeze to death, I told Scotty and Dan the next time I saw them. She had loved her time in the woods, cinched in her sleeping bag, reading and relishing the solitude. But by the time I mentioned this, neither remembered whom I was talking about or why I was telling them. We did better mining the past.

The Methodist service where Scotty's vocal enthusiasm found welcome was a monthly occurrence at County, in the activities room that became a makeshift sanctuary for an hour or two, and there were frequent Episcopal and Catholic services, too. The denomination seemed to be beside the point. I saw Catholics at the Methodist service, and Methodists at the Episcopal one, and the occasional Jew might show up, too. Going to church was something to do, yes, but so was "Classic Morning Movie," and often church had better attendance. Possibly, and inadvertently, churchgoers at County were drawn not only by the liturgy and the music, but also by what happened to them when they came together to listen to them: they got happy. It turns out that older people who attend religious services are more likely to view life positively and less likely to have symptoms of depression. This is true across the religious spectrum; religious affiliation is not a factor.

For County residents, too, it seemed, going to church, singing hymns, and listening to a homily were less about doctrine and more about the comfort that comes from ritual, connection, and familiarity. It was religion writ large, religion in its essence, and sometimes, walking down the hallway with Pransky as "Go Tell It on the Mountain" and "Amazing Grace" leaked out of the activities room, I wondered if the solace those folks found there was really what faith was about. The dictionary also said that faith was "a strong belief in God or in the doctrines of a religion," but that seemed too narrow. In the Epistle to the Hebrews, the anonymous New Testament author put it this way: "Faith is confidence in what we hope for and assurance about what we don't see" (Hebrews 11:1). It's a lovely thought, though the rationalists among us use it as evidence that the whole enterprise is silly and made up. The simple formulation of this argument is that faith is in conflict with reason, and that faith comes from some earlier, less evolved, and less sophisticated time, a time before science. And while this argument certainly makes sense, it misses the point. "In general, believing in, as distinguished from believing that, marks the distinction between religious faith and scientific belief or opinion," the twentieth-century philosopher Herbert Wallace Schneider wrote in 1924. "When faith is viewed under the category of hope . . . its subject matter shifts from our ground of assurance in the existence or reality of a thing, to our willingness to look forward to it as an object of our interest or endeavor." At the nursing home, unseen things, whether they were in the mind's eye, which was focused on what may or may not have been, or embedded in visions of a future that did not resemble what was, were not uncommon. Clyde, for instance, was certain his nephew would be arriving any day with the keys to a red classic Mustang convertible so he could finally move back to his trailer home in Florida as soon as the tenant there moved out. His wasn't a religious faith, though he said it with conviction and so often that it was obvious that he believed it and that it kept him going.

'm not sure where the unforeseen fits in with the unseen in matters of faith, but there were days when things happened at the nursing home that were so unexpected they seemed miraculous. There's a whole branch of spirituality that trades in angels and miracles, and what I witnessed at County, sometimes because of the dog, and sometimes simply because the dog had brought me there, was not like that at all. There were no burning bushes or parting seas the morning Thomas spoke, there was only his voice and his words and the active mind I'd assumed did not exist. The miracle wasn't his—he'd been able to speak all along—it was mine. Call it the miracle of enlightenment. Or, better still, call it the miracle of waking up to not writing people off.

For weeks, when Pransky and I visited Thomas, our encounters always went the same way. Thomas, dressed in a stained polo shirt and sweats, would be sitting in the dayroom, looking at the TV. The dog and I would approach, Thomas would reach out with his left hand, and with fingers callused from a life of milking cows and mending fences, zero in on a particular spot on Pransky's back, and move those fingers methodically in and out, like he was clenching and releasing his fist. It was a simple transaction, but one that appeared to bring both parties great pleasure. Thomas said nothing. I said nothing. Sometimes Pranny would sigh. After about five minutes, Thomas would withdraw his hand and we'd move on.

"She likes that," Thomas said one morning, unbidden. I was shocked. "You can speak!" I wanted to exclaim, but I restrained myself and instead said enthusiastically, "She does!"

"She got a haircut," he added. Not only could he speak, he'd been paying attention.

"So what are you watching?" I asked. On the screen was a tanned, buff, pleasantly handsome man in crisp blue scrubs sitting on a stool on a stage looking out at a studio audience. He was the quintessence of the television medicine man. Clyde, who had rolled up next to Thomas, was watching, too.

"Doctors talking," Thomas said. He had a shambling way of speaking that was more articulate than a mumble, but barely. "About health things." It seemed a bit coals-to-Newcastle-busman's-holidayish to me that a couple of guys who were endlessly prodded and poked by people in scrubs—though none as unwrinkled as the one on TV—would want to spend their free time listening to white coats talk about kidneys and prostates, but both men were giving the screen their undivided attention. Was it that the fellow on TV was an actual physician—or at least an actor playing one—while the people who worked at County were mainly nurses' aides, LPNs, and RNs? This was, after all, a nursing home, which is to say that most of the people who worked there were nurses. The doctors were all across the street at the hospital, with the high-tech MRI machines and CT scanners and the money. I don't mean this cynically or abstractly. When the hospital board decided to close its end-of-life, palliative care practice, which was composed of the only two doctors I ever saw at County, and those rarely, it was because the meat-and-potatoes of palliative care—keeping patients comfortable, relieving their pain, and guiding them as gently as possible out of this life—generates only gristle. Without lots of machine-driven tests, labs, and surgical interventions, which were where the real money was, the hospital board chair told the local newspaper, the practice wasn't viable. Plain old doctoring, in other words, just did not pay.

"So what's this show about?" I asked after the commercial break, when the handsome male doctor—think: plastic surgeon—was joined onstage by a gorgeous female doctor—think: dermatologist. (And yes, think: not fair, those are stereotypes.) Which is to say I was expecting the answer to be "calf implants" or "varicose vein reduction." This was, after all, daytime TV.

"It's taboo," Thomas said, and before I had a chance to consider all dimensions of this unlikely response, Clyde said, "Sex." Clyde was looking right at me when he said the word, like he was trying to see if I'd blink. Or, Clyde being Clyde, maybe this was his idea of a pickup line.

"What about sex?" I asked innocently.

"Contraception," Thomas said.

"Booorrring," Clyde said, "blah, blah, blah," and he unlocked the brakes on his wheelchair and spun himself down the hall toward the activities room, where a bunch of residents and volunteers were busy making corn-husk dolls. He liked to be where the ladies were.

Of course, just by being at County, Clyde was where the ladies were—especially the ladies his own age, the over-eighty crowd. In part, this was simple statistics. Women live, on average, four-plus years longer than men, though as recently as 1980, the gap was much greater—almost eight years. Still, those four years were significant. They meant that there were many more older women in the population at large than older men, and that by age eighty-five, there were three women for every man. Add to this the facts that 72 percent of nursing home residents were women, and that elderly women were more likely to end up in a nursing home than elderly men, and Clyde was in a ladies' man's paradise—depending on one's definition of paradise. According to one government report on gender differences in nursing homes, older women were most "at risk" of a nursing home placement, a turn of phrase that accurately reflects the way most people feel about facilities like the county nursing home. They were places of last resort.

One day, when Pransky and I were emerging from the room of a woman on the rehabilitation wing whose drinking had taken such a toll on her diabetes that she was in danger of losing her leg, and who told me it was not true, no matter what the visiting nurses said, she wasn't abusing her Percocet and Vicodin, and who cried when she saw my dog because she missed her dog so much, and who wondered how much we were paid to walk around County and visit people because maybe that was a job she could get, too, although it would be hard to get over to the nursing home since her license had been taken away, we ran into Nelson Rutherford, County's chief administrator.

"This must be Pransky," he said, bending down and addressing her directly. "She looks like a very nice dog."

"She is a nice dog," I said.

"So how do you like it here?" he asked.

"It's a really nice place," I said. "We like it." I went on to explain that I liked it because it was friendly and clean, and that Pransky liked it because residents were constantly slipping her table scraps that they'd save for days, anticipating her visit.

"What if you had to live here, would you still like it?" he asked. It was the unspoken question, the one I'd asked myself many times, especially when I'd hear myself telling friends that County was nothing like those depressing nursing homes that were portrayed in the media, but it was surprising to hear it asked out loud by the nursing home's director.

"See," he said, when I didn't answer right away. "That's the problem. Baby boomers won't want to be here, right?" he said. "I'm a baby boomer myself, and this is not what I would want for myself. That's why we're trying to make it more like a home. Which is why it's good to see a dog here."

While it was flattering to think that Pransky and I were changing the ambience at County, making a nursing home more homelike was a tall order that wouldn't begin to be filled even with ten dogs walking the corridors. (Though that would be pretty entertaining.) That institutions like County were called "homes" was not because they'd ever been cozy domiciles but because they descended from eighteenth-century almshouses and poorhouses, places so vile they were intended to discourage the destitute, many of whom were old and sick, from taking up residence there. In the twentieth century, at the height of the Great Depression, when President Roosevelt signed the Social Security Act, he recognized the precarious position many older folks found themselves in by establishing old age assistance for retired workers. The problem was that the same law also mandated that old folks couldn't collect those benefits if they were living in any sort of public facility, like a poorhouse. The new law had the dual effect of shutting down the almshouses and giving rise to private care facilities where the elderly could spend the subsistence money the government gave them. But those places were no better than their predecessors, so in 1950 the government tried again, this time establishing standards of care for nursing homes and lifting the rule that banned people getting old age assistance from using their benefits in publicly funded places. Four years later the government took this one step further, authorizing grants to encourage the construction of nursing facilities that would be affiliated with hospitals. The home model was out; after 1954, nursing homes began to be "medicalized." As that happened, nursing homes migrated out of the welfare system and into the health-care system. They were homes in name only.

The 1954 law was followed by a series of other reforms, each one intended to rectify problems arising from the reform that preceded it. It was like dominoes in reverse, with new laws to fix the poor standard of care, minimal oversight, and funding issues that seemed to plague nursing homes everywhere, public and private. While each iteration of the law was intended to improve care, taken together they reinforced the public's perception that nursing homes were squalid, scary, underfunded, monstrous places. That County was none of these things was, in part, because it was a public institution in a small, community-minded town, and there was a lot of foot traffic in and out, from family and friends, volunteers, and high school and college students. The parking lot was almost always full; the door was always open. Musicians stopped by regularly—it wasn't unusual to see a harpist setting up, or to hear bluegrass or chamber music from down the hall. People dropped off books, puzzles, movies, and clothes. They came to assemble gingerbread houses at Christmas, and carve pumpkins at Halloween. It seemed to be a rule that no holiday could go uncelebrated at County. (One late morning, I found Scotty and Dan in the activities room, happily gnawing on spareribs and cracking open fortune cookies. "What's the occasion?" I asked. "Chinese New Year," Scotty said. "Year of the chicken," Dan added.) People were proud of County the way they were proud of the local hospital, both of which were not what you might expect to find in a town of less than ten thousand people. Recently, the nursing home had been named the region's best nonprofit business of the year, and there was a banner staked in the parking lot median announcing this.

The other reason County wasn't one of those scary nursing homes had to do with the hospital. County was built on the hospital campus, just like the authors of the 1954 law had imagined, and that was a good thing for the quality of care, the cleanliness, and the professionalism of the staff. But it was a bad thing if what you wanted was to make the place more like a home. Sterile and antiseptic were reassuring, but they weren't inviting, and dog or no dog, Nelson, the director, knew it.

"The twenty-first-century nursing home can't look like the twentieth-century nursing home," Nelson said, and began to lay out his vision of what that "culture change," as he was calling it, would be: separate units of about eight or ten residents apiece, where each resident would have his or her own suite, built around a common area. It would be more private than the hospital model, and more communal, with staff coming in and out as needed.

In theory it sounded nice, but when I tried to imagine Joe and Dottie and Vinny and Iris and Clyde and Thomas and Lizzie and Fran living in one of these nursing home villas, I couldn't do it. When Joe got depressed he wouldn't come out of his room, Fran had a hard time getting out of bed even when she was feeling well, Lizzie and Thomas were not especially interactive, Iris had trouble speaking, Dottie couldn't hear, Vinny could be prickly and only wanted to talk college sports, and Clyde was, well, Clyde. In any case, theory was likely to be as far as this idea got, since County was already stretched thin financially and building a new facility did not seem like it would be in the cards anytime soon. Instead, Nelson said, culture change at County would have to happen incrementally. It would start with putting hardwood floors in the dining room to give it a more elegant ambience, and then reserving a corner for what the director was calling "the coffee shop," where residents and visitors could hang out and chat and play cards and drink from an endless pot of coffee. The idea that these two adjustments would someday lead to a different kind of nursing home—now, that was faith.

Stella and Marlene were not waiting for culture change. They had made their room on West homier than most homes. The walls were covered with county fair ribbons for Stella's squash and cucumbers, which she grew in the courtyard garden in beds that had been built to wheelchair height, and with her paintings, some on black velvet, the kind that came from kits. There were wood carvings, embroidered pillows, stuffed animals, books, magazines, snow globes, and statuary covering every other available space. And that was only on her side of the room, which was spare compared with Marlene's. Marlene's side was filled, almost to overflowing, with dolls and stuffed animals. They covered the bed, the windowsill, the bookcase, and the floor in front of the bookcase. They were lined, three deep, against the radiator. If I wanted to sit down, I'd have to move bears and elephants and a hedgehog. It took Marlene ten minutes at night to move the day residents off her bed, and ten minutes in the morning to reverse the task. Her half of the room was a child's paradise, and one day, when my two-year-old friend Ella was making the rounds with me and Pranny, Marlene handed her a dancing, singing pig that so delighted her, she wouldn't leave. Ella just kept pushing the button, the pig just kept singing "Everything is beautiful, in its own way," and from the other side of the room Stella joined in, which delighted Ella even more.

Having Ella with me was a revelation. More than once she charged ahead and wandered into someone's room—anyone's room—and by the time I'd caught up with her she was charming the person in the bed. Nothing bothered her—not bandages, not wheelchairs, not a person's wrinkled and mottled skin. She made no distinctions based on incapacities or physical appearance. Everyone was interesting to her; no one was frightening or off-putting. She was like the dog, taking everyone as they came—frail, fat, inaudible, crippled, whatever—without judgment.

Watching the two of them, it occurred to me that maybe innocence is lost when we stop seeing people for who they are (in this case, a random assortment of elders) and see them for what they are—disabled, aphasic, blind, mute. Then we let ourselves think of them as not "normal" and, therefore, "other." Neither Pransky nor Ella understood "other." Neither looked at Stella, whose wounded legs were bandaged toe to knee, and assumed she was her legs. Stella had a beautiful singing voice, she was a crafter, she was friendly, but these were not what Ella and Pransky saw, either. For them the attraction was more elemental. It wasn't about anything. They started from acceptance, unlike the rest of us.

And the truth was, Stella could be prickly. She was often on the lookout for problems and was never shy about complaining, which the staff did not always appreciate, while the residents almost always did: they elected her head of the residents' council, which was like student government at County. Marlene, on the other hand, was so sunny that her eyes had grown squinty from what appeared to be the permanent smile on her face. Like Iris and Dottie, Stella and Marlene had come in as strangers years ago and now were like an old married couple, able to negotiate their small space without much friction.

Sometimes Pranny and I would walk in and Stella would be watching a game show on her TV and, not more than three feet away, Marlene would be watching a soap opera on hers, and both seemed content. But other times they'd be sitting next to each other in the activities room, playing bingo, or cutting apples for pie, or sharing applesauce recipes. They both attended the Catholic church service, too, and I sometimes wondered if it was the things they had in common before they ever met—their Catholic upbringings in the New York City area, their marriages to men who had served in the Navy during World War II—that let them settle into an easy alliance.

Organized religion, which can seem so fundamentally divisive, can also collapse our six degrees of separation to zero. It's only the most unimaginative literalist who thinks that the brother in "my brother's keeper" is a blood relation, but no one doubts he is a relation. That's how it seemed with Stella and Marlene—like they were connected, even when one was focused on *Wheel of Fortune* and the other on *Days of Our Lives*. They knew things about each other without those things ever having been said, and they would have known them even if they'd never known each other. I suppose, on a basic level, that's what happened when you said the same prayers in the same order week after week—not because you knew them by heart, and not even because they had significance, but because it was a shared experience. Even if you were in different churches, in different states or different countries, the routine bound you, one to the other. And once it did, and you knew you had that in common, you could make assumptions about each other, which was another way of sharing. And the connection went beyond whatever happened inside a sanctuary, and maybe didn't have anything to do with a sanctuary, because other people made assumptions about you, too, which strengthened your bonds and what you knew about each other.

Then there was Fran. She seemed fundamentally alone but unbothered by this; she appeared to be thoroughly self-possessed. Yet her mind was so active that her confinement seemed cruel—not her confinement at County so much as the confinement imposed by her failing body.

"The growth on my bladder isn't cancer," she said one morning when the blue jays and squirrels were vying for the seeds in her feeder and Pransky was watching intently from her ringside seat at the end of Fran's bed. I had had no idea that she had a growth on her bladder, and while it not being cancerous was obviously good news, the real

point was that Fran had some sort of growth on her bladder that was making her uncomfortable.

Another time I brought her a book, only to learn that
her eyes had clouded over so that she saw everything
through a white haze, as if she lived engulfed in a cloud of
smoke. Reading was nearly impossible. So was looking at
photos. When she watched her beloved Red Sox on TV,
she was really just listening. She could stand up, and she
could walk with a walker, but it was slow going, and her
arthritic fingers had a hard time wrapping around the
handles.

"I can hardly hear out of my left ear anymore," Fran
mentioned one day. This was in addition to her fuzzy eyes
and bad stomach. "The Red Sox aren't doing so well,
either," she added, "but they are paid a lot more not to do
well."

If the French philosopher Descartes needed an object
example to prove his point that mind and body are separate entitics, he would not do better than to choose Fran.
As her body attacked itself, as it wasted away, as it stalled,
her mind was as robust as ever. Though she had trouble
reading the newspaper, she started a current-events club
at County, and when, after a few weeks, it became clear
that she was its only member, she didn't give up, but

instead conducted meetings from her bed, as the volunteer moderator, a local schoolteacher, summarized articles from *The New York Times* and *The Boston Globe*.

"What do you think about the new Facebook privacy rules?" Fran might ask me, even though I was pretty sure she'd never seen Facebook, nor had any interest in seeing it, either. Or, "It seems like that actress Lindsay Lohan is on a path of self-destruction," and, "Do you think it's fair that the Olympics won't allow women's ski jumping?" Fran's mind was unfettered, and when she was in conversation she could escape her body; she could travel. So the morning the blind minister wandered in, holding a Bible in one hand and a red-tipped cane in the other, I was surprised, and then embarrassed, by Fran's reaction. She shut down. Her voice became tight, her answers monosyllabic. She was pointedly uninterested.

The minister's name was Paul, and he was a friendly man, a graduate of Harvard, somebody told me when I'd met him a few weeks earlier during his stay on the rehab wing. Now he was back, trolling the halls, a pastor in search of a congregation.

"How are you doing today?" he asked Fran.

"Fine," she said, with more than a hint of acid in her voice.

"That's good, that's good," the minister said. He appeared to be not only blind but also deaf to her antagonism. "Is there anything you'd like to talk about this morning?"

"No," she said, her body rigid, her jaw barely moving.

"No concerns?" He tried again.

"No."

"How are you feeling?"

"You already asked that."

"Right," he said patiently. The smile he had carried into the room had not abated, and now he stood there dumbly, as Fran stewed in her bed.

"I don't know if you realize this, but I have guests," Fran said, a little meanly, since this was clearly meant to remind him that he couldn't see. She did not bother to tell him that one of her guests was, at that very moment, in bed with her and was a dog. "Guests," plural, sounded more authoritative than "guest."

"Okay, then," he said. "Maybe next time."

"There will be no next time," Fran growled when he finally left and it was just the three of us again on her side of the room. "Why can he just walk in here, uninvited?" she said. And it was funny—nurses and aides and housekeepers were walking in and out of there, uninvited, day and night, and Fran welcomed them. But an itinerant minister eager to listen to her concerns offended her deeply. At the time I didn't think this had anything to do with religion itself, but later, when I found out that Fran was descended from a seventeenth-century Puritan-turned-Quaker who believed that God spoke directly to individuals without need of clergy, and who was hung in Boston for her beliefs, I wondered if Fran's antipathy for the minister wasn't inborn. It was as good a theory as any, but I suspected her anger was less historical than it was emotional; she had been humiliated. Paul's easy access reminded Fran just where and what she was: an invalid confined to a piece of real estate that was no more than a few square feet—her bed. Even though Fran's frailty was on twenty-four-hour display, Paul's presence, and Fran's inability to escape it, blasted away any illusions of autonomy that she had been able to construct about herself. He could have been anybody—the door was open; she was not getting out of that bed—but the fact that he wasn't just anyone, but someone who used his clerical collar like a hall pass, ticked her off. But that was only part of it. What was worse was that I had witnessed her helplessness, and her loss of dignity, and it embarrassed us both.

Once Paul left, we used the dog as a foil, talking about

hunting season, which was coming up, and how Pransky disliked the blaze-orange jacket we made her wear when there were people roaming the woods with rifles, and a few other inconsequential things, till it was easy for the dog and me to make our exit without it seeming related to what I'd seen there, even though it was obvious to me and to Fran, too, that that was exactly why we were leaving. Whatever holiday from sickness that Pranny and I had provided Fran was over.

A week later, when Pransky and I arrived at Fran's door, it was closed. Typically doors were kept open, shut only when catheters were being changed or medicine was administered. I could have knocked, but I was chicken; maybe the whole Paul thing had blown over, but maybe it hadn't. "This isn't about us," I said to Pranny, who had come to expect a turn on Fran's bed each week, though I was pretty sure it was. How else could a person confined to bed assert her autonomy and restore her dignity? This was not a rhetorical question.

The next week Fran's door was open, but the curtain was drawn all the way around her bed, so she was out of sight. This time, though, I knocked and told her I was there with Pransky. Did she want a visit? No, she said, she wasn't feeling well.

"Should we come back next week?" I called out to her.

"You can try," she said.

"Come on, Pranny," I said to my dog, who was already making her way into Fran's room. I pulled on her leash a bit to stop her, and she looked back over her shoulder, confused, but perked up when I told her we were going to visit the Carters. The Carters, Mr. and Mrs., lived a few doors down from Fran. They kept a box of dog biscuits in their cupboard.

would like to report that the next time Pransky and I approached Fran's door it was open, and the curtain was pulled back, and as soon as Fran saw us she waved us into the room, patting her mattress so Pran would know it was okay to jump up. I'd also like to report that things were back to where they'd been almost a month earlier, which is to say that Fran was her old, inquisitive self and wanted me to explain Justin Bieber. As it turned out, when we got to her room the door was open and Fran's roommate was not there and neither was Fran. It was eerie: the window shades were up and the sun was pouring in and the beds were undisturbed. It crossed my mind that one or the other of them had died, but just as quickly that thought was replaced with the understanding that someone would have told me.

"Where's Fran?" I asked the first aide I saw, but she had no idea.

"Where's Fran?" I asked someone else. And someone else. Not even the people who looked like they should know knew. Fran was one of our favorite people at County—mine and Pransky's. She wasn't sweet, like Marlene. She wasn't grandmotherly, like Iris. Fran was a tough old bird with a sharp eye and a sharper wit, and now she was gone. I knew I liked Fran, but I hadn't realized how much I looked forward to sitting opposite her as she and Pransky got comfortable in her bed. There was a certain amount of transience at County, and even for long-term residents like Fran, it was not more than a way station between this life and whatever came next. Most of the time that was possible to ignore. This was not one of those times.

was at the eye doctor's." Fran laughed when we saw her the following week. Pransky had been restored to her place in the bed, and Fran was upbeat and full of questions, and whatever strangeness had come between us was either gone or hadn't been there in the first place. Had I been projecting?

"I'm going to have to ask you to leave," she said after we'd been there about ten minutes. "I have to get dressed. I'm going out to lunch."

"Wow!" I said. Sometimes it was hard to remember that County residents were adults, free to come and go as they pleased. "Where?"

"My friend is taking me to the A&W," Fran said. "There is nothing like a good hot dog with mustard and relish. Sorry, Pran."

"It's okay," I said. "She'd eat a dog in a heartbeat, though I'm not sure about the mustard."

When we passed by Fran's room again, close to noon, she was gone.

The last image I have of Fran is from behind, walking out the door of the nursing home pushing her walker, wearing sneakers, slacks, and her Red Sox sweatshirt. If she wasn't smiling, it was only because of the effort it took to propel that thing over the threshold.

Early in the morning, exactly a week later, after a night of labored breathing, Fran went through those doors again, this time on a stretcher, which was loaded into an ambulance for the one-minute ride to the hospital. The doctors diagnosed pneumonia. She was put in the ICU.

"I'd like to go over there," I told the nursing home chaplain. She said she'd find out if I could.

I'd like to think that if I'd known Fran was going to die, I would have made it a point to see her in the hospital, to say goodbye and thank her for welcoming Pransky and me into her world. But when the chaplain called that afternoon, I wasn't home, and the next day there didn't seem to be a minute to spare, and since I knew I was going to be near the hospital the following morning for a meeting, I decided to wait and go then. Fran died before sunrise.

This was in the fall. Months later, after the ground had thawed and the snow had returned to the earth and sky, Fran was to be buried in a small cemetery on a hillside that pointed to the mountains. "The service is on Saturday," the chaplain told me. "I thought you'd want to know."

Was she thinking I'd want to go? Was she asking me to go? Did I belong there? What if nobody showed up?

got to the cemetery minutes before the service started and was surprised to see thirty people gathered on the hillside and more converging from left and right, walking toward them. Pransky was on the leash; it seemed appropriate to do this together. Who were these people, I wondered, and how were they related to Fran? Whatever narrative I had imposed on her spinster life, it didn't include scores of people moved to attend her funeral, since by the time the service started there must have been nearly fifty people there.

I hung back with Pransky, worried that it might seem disrespectful to everyone except Fran to have come with a dog to her burial. The others stood in a semicircle around the grave site as the nursing home chaplain conducted the service. Some of them held hands. Downwind, I was having trouble hearing the words, so I thought about Fran, and how feisty and brave and open to the world she was, and how, even when the parameters of her physical world shrank and shrank and shrank some more, she was undiminished. The words "Fran" and "prayer" and "join" had just drifted down to me when, in unison, the makeshift congregation began to speak as one, saying:

God grant me the serenity
to accept the things I cannot change;
courage to change the things I can;
and wisdom to know the difference
Living one day at a time,
Enjoying one day at a time,
Accepting hardship as a pathway to peace,
Taking, as Jesus did,
The sinful world as it is,
Not as I would have it,
Trusting that You will make all things right,
If I surrender to Your will,
So that I may be reasonably happy in this life,
And supremely happy with You in the next.
Amen.

It was the Serenity Prayer, spoken by members of Alcoholics Anonymous at the beginning of every meeting. In an earlier part of her life, after stints as a reporter and a public-relations executive, Fran had been a drug and alcohol counselor. And it dawned on me—call it a revelation: these were her people; they were her church. "Most of them had parents who were abusers, so it was a pretty futile exercise," Fran told me when I asked about her work, but it turned out she was wrong. It turned out that she had been rock and redeemer.

4.

Fortitude

hen Pransky got sick, very, very sick—not sick like Fran, whose ailments were constant, rude, unshakable companions, but sick, as the saying goes, as a dog. We like to think that we understand our animals, and that they understand us, and that this understanding is the basis of our *very special* relationship. Our dog "gets" us; we "get" the dog. And most of the time, because we are both creatures of habit, and because what we ask of them (loyalty, fealty, love) and what they

ask of us (loyalty, fealty, love, and food) is straightforward and uncomplicated, all that getting is got. Then the
dog gets sick, or seems to be sick, or is just not herself,
and you are reminded in the worst way, at the worst
time, how limited your understanding really is. I've
heard experts say that dogs are capable of achieving the
comprehension of a five-year-old child, whatever that
means, but when your dog is sick, one thing it means is
that your five-year-old never learned how to talk. When
you ask her "Where does it hurt?" for example, you're
likely to get a plaintive stare—plaintive being your interpretation of her unknowable expression.

Pransky's illness came on very suddenly, though
maybe it had been brewing. I had been away for a few
days, and Bill and Sophie had been off together in the
Adirondack Mountains, swimming and hiking and doing
summery things. I would have joined them there, but
every July County threw a big barbecue for residents,
family, friends, and staff in the courtyard, with burgers
on the grill and ice cream and watermelon and music and
games, and I wanted to go with Pransky, who didn't
know she wanted to go, but would when she got there
and people started sneaking her pieces of grilled meat.

This year's theme was baseball, specifically Red Sox versus Yankees. For weeks, residents and staff had been asked to declare an allegiance to one or the other team, and once they had, Janie or Carol would take their picture wearing their team's baseball cap and turn the picture into a trading card. The bulletin board outside the activities room was filled with pictures—Scotty as a Yankee, Iris as a Red Sox slugger. Pransky got her picture taken, too, with a Red Sox cap tilted jauntily to the side, so that it covered one eye and rested on her snout. She looked fetching, which was appropriate, since the highlight of the event was to be a Yankees–Sox Wiffle-ball game, with Pransky slated to be the Sox's utility outfielder. Our team definitely had the age advantage: one member was ninety-eight years old.

So this was the day, and I'd taken the red-eye to Albany in order to get to the nursing home on time. The plan was to meet Bill along the way and do a switch: dog and child would come with me, while Bill drove on to the airport for his own quick trip out of town. All was going well. The plane was on time, my car started, Albany was free of traffic, and Bill, coming from the north, arrived at the designated meet-up point just as I pulled in from the south. It was a few minutes after nine in the morning.

"Pransky is not feeling well," Bill said when he greeted me. He pointed to the backseat of his car, where Pranny was stretched out, door to door, with her head hanging off the side like she was seasick. She thumped her tail once when she heard my voice, but made no effort to get up. This was not good. It was not normal. Pransky was an enthusiast. Give her an excuse to wag her tail and she'd take it. The car door was open. Under normal circumstances she would have jumped out by now, but she hadn't budged. Then Bill said that she had thrown up a few times overnight, and I was strangely mollified. Whoever in the history of idioms had paired the word "fortitude" with the word "intestinal" had not met our dog. She—literally—had none. It was nothing serious, the vet told us, suggesting that we might want to shop in the "sensitive stomach" dog food aisle at the feed store.

"She can still go to the Wiffle-ball game, right?" I asked, and though I posed this as a question, I didn't want it to be. I had been looking forward to this for weeks. I had driven half the night to get to an airport that could get me back in time. I really, really wanted to go, and I really, really wanted to take Pransky, and I wanted

Sophie to be there, too. There was precedent, I reminded Bill: when Sophie was four we took her to Shea Stadium for a Mets game after she'd spent the morning throwing up, and that had worked out all right.

"Ask Pranny if she wants to play Wiffle ball," I said to Sophie, who had moved into the backseat with the dog and was stroking her flank.

"She does not want to play Wiffle ball, Mom," Sophie said, stating the obvious.

"Maybe she's just tired," Bill suggested.

"From throwing up all night," Sophie added. It was clear that she thought she was the only adult in the vicinity, which was probably true.

Bill handed me the leash and retrieved a bag of dog food from the trunk. It was something generic and definitely not from the sensitive-stomach aisle of Agway or any other store.

"What's this?" I asked.

"We ran out of food," Bill explained, "so I got it at the supermarket." And then he clapped, once, loudly, and urged Pransky to get up and get out, and being a good dog, she stood, stretched, and jumped out of his car and into mine in what seemed to be a single fluid motion. Sick dogs can't do that, I told myself. The nursing home was forty-six miles away. If we left now, we'd still be on time. "Maybe she'll sleep it off," I said, and put the car in gear.

It was a pleasant drive on a perfect, warm, blue-sky summer's day, punctuated every so often with me asking Sophie to turn around and check on the dog.

"How is she?" I'd ask.

"The same," she'd say, and then we went back to talking about whatever we had been talking about.

"Do you think she could have gotten into something?" I asked, knowing this was an impossible question to answer. Sophie, Bill, and Pranny had been hiking; they had been swimming. When she was outside, Pransky liked to follow her nose, and sometimes her nose yielded edible treasures: frogs, squirrels, rabbits, and once the entire unstrung rib cage of a deer—and these were just the ones we knew about.

"Are we still going to the nursing home?" Sophie asked a few times.

"I guess we'll see when we get closer," I'd say, though, of course, each time she asked we were closer, and Pransky was still sacked out in the backseat. And then we were in range, ten miles away, and it seemed like a good idea to stop the car, take the dog for a walk, and assess. Head-on, I had to admit, she did not look good. Her nose was a dry, faded gray, and her eyes seemed a bit glazed, but when I opened her door she got right up, her tail aloft, and there was no hesitation in her step. If Sophie had asked me, right then, if we were going to go to County, I would have said yes.

But she didn't ask. Instead she had taken the leash and was walking Pransky over to a small strip of grass at the edge of the asphalt where we'd parked. Reaching it, the dog immediately squatted, I thought, to pee.

There are moments in life that serve as markers separating before and after, and sometimes they are not obvious except in retrospect; like when you find out that the pain you began to feel in March was really the beginning of the cancer that was diagnosed in September. Other times they are immediate: like when you're hit from behind while idling at a traffic light. This time, with Pransky, was like that. I looked down at her expecting to see one thing, and the thing I saw caused my heart to race and my mouth to begin to repeat the words "oh my God," involuntarily, at least five times, because fear had stolen every other word. Blood, deep-red blood, was pouring out of her rear end as if someone had opened a faucet.

"She's bleeding internally," I managed to say. "We have to get her to the animal hospital right away."

The animal hospital, like the nursing home, was at least a fifteen-minute and probably a twenty-minute drive over crummy, rutted, narrow roads, and suddenly, out of nowhere, it seemed possible that we might lose Pransky before we could get her there. Pransky was just about eight years old. Eight was not old for a medium-sized dog, but it was not young, either. If she died at eight she would have had a good, full life, but since less than twenty-four hours earlier she had seemed to be gloriously and uninhibitedly in the thick of that life, this turn of events seemed especially cruel.

"What's going to happen?" Sophie asked—meaning "Is she going to die?"

"I don't know," I said. "This can't be good."

We were back in the car by then, driving too fast, as I worked to stay focused on the road, keeping an eye out for stray cows, stray cats, and other people's dogs, every mile or so asking Sophie, who was turned around in her seat and holding one of Pranny's paws, how Pran was doing, till even I found myself annoying, though I couldn't stop. Sophie's other hand held our cell phone, which was useless—this was rural Vermont, and there was no service.

"How many bars?" I'd ask when I wasn't asking for an update on Pransky's condition.

"None," she'd say without looking. Our entire vocabulary had been reduced to about a dozen words.

The thing about dogs—the worst thing about dogs—is that they are always dying. Even when they live relatively long lives, those lives are too short: the average life expectancy for a North American dog is about thirteen years, and that includes little dogs, like Jack Russell terriers, that typically live longer, and hefty ones, like the Bernese mountain dog, that are lucky to get to ten. Sophie, at sixteen, had already buried two dogs. The possibility that she might bury a third was unthinkable—even though it was on both our minds. The cratering loss experienced when a dog dies is different from the cratering loss experienced when other loved ones die because the whole relationship, at its core, is about nothing but mutual trust, a trust that is elemental, direct, and uncomplicated. The death of a dog feels like a failure. It feels like goodness itself has been extinguished.

"Two bars," Sophie said when we were about three miles from the animal hospital, and without asking, got the number, dialed it, and put the phone up to my ear.

"My dog has an emergency," I said, and before the receptionist could ask if it was okay to put me on hold I told her that Pransky appeared to be bleeding internally. I said this as calmly and matter-of-factly as I could, channeling the lessons learned from the many television medical dramas I'd seen where the person making the call was too distraught to speak intelligibly. That, and I didn't want to alarm my daughter—or, for that matter, myself. "We need to come in right now," I added.

"Do you have an appointment?" the receptionist asked.

"What?"

"Do you have an appointment?" she said again.

I could feel my medical-drama persona about to be strangled by my true, terrified, and now furious self. "Of course we don't have an appointment," I said. "It's an emergency." We were, by then, less than a mile away, and I told her so. "We will be there in five minutes," I said. "Maybe three. We need to see a doctor right away."

A few minutes later, Pransky walked into the vet's office on her own four feet. Her tail was between her legs, but it always was when she visited the place where nice people in white coats kneeled at eye level, talked to her in dulcet tones, and then stuck a needle in her back.

"And who do we have here?" the receptionist said in her jolly, singsongy way.

"Pransky," I said. "We just called. We're the emergency." As I said this, a portly man with glasses and facial hair stepped out of one of the examining rooms and waved us in. He looked to be in his early forties, and resembled an overfed mastiff. I'd never seen him before. I gave him Pransky's leash. When I thought about this later, it seemed remarkable how willing most of us are to hand over ourselves or our loved ones to complete strangers to be healed, and how it's better that they are complete strangers, since it's easier to believe, then, that they may be shamans.

The vet put Pransky on the scale. Two weeks before, when she had come in for her annual checkup, she'd weighed forty-seven pounds. Now she was down to forty-one. And she was shaking. Her whole body was vibrating like a rattle. The vet shined a light into her eyes and down her throat. He picked up her earflaps and peered into the dark canals underneath. He palpated her stomach, then lifted her tail and did something with his gloved finger that made her squeal. He drew vials of blood, as if she had plenty to spare, which seemed unlikely. He hummed under his breath, not a song but a sound that began and ended in "mm." Pransky made the same sound sometimes in her sleep. He put his stethoscope on her belly, then moved it around.

"I'm not hearing anything too strange," he said after a while.

"That's good," I said. "Right?"

"Mm. Mmm."

"Did she eat anything out of the ordinary?" he asked. I said I had been away, but I didn't think so, though of course we couldn't be sure.

"But no," I said, and at the same time Sophie said, "Yes." The doctor and I both turned to look in her direction. She was in the far corner of the room, where Pransky had retreated as soon as the vet let her down from the examining table. "Don't you remember?" Sophie said to me. "The dog food Dad gave you? The stuff from the supermarket?"

The doctor arched his eyebrows. "A sudden change in diet is known to cause gastrointestinal bleeding," he said.

It seemed unlikely. We had changed Pransky's food before without blood pouring out of her. If this was a known complication, why didn't it say so on the dog-food bag? And why didn't everyone know about it, like they knew about dogs and chocolate, or dogs and grapes? "You're saying that just by eating a cup of strange dog food . . ." My voice trailed off. The whole thing was too far-fetched, and too easy. I had walked in there convinced my dog was dying and it was going to take a better explanation than this one to reassure me that she wasn't.

"I'm saying that changing the food can greatly irritate the intestinal tract, and if the irritation is severe it can cause bleeding," he explained. He went on to say that it was good that we had caught it early, and that once we withdrew the source of the irritation, the bleeding would stop."

"So she's not dying?" I ventured.

"She's not dying, but she is very uncomfortable," he said. "Her stomach hurts and she's dehydrated and has lost a lot of blood. No food for twenty-four hours, and then I want you to feed her small pieces of chicken and boiled white rice. Start with a quarter-cup, and over the course of the week, gradually get it up to two cups." He also ordered an ultrasound of her abdomen, in case something else was going on, and bed rest. As for the nursing home, she was grounded for at least two weeks. Too many germs and too many people eager to slip her contraband. Just the week before, Clyde, who was probably right at that very moment getting up to bat for the County Yankees, had offered her a pink sugar wafer cookie, the kind held together by a mortar of thick white icing, that I intercepted just as he was about to make the handoff. He was not pleased and neither was Pransky, but I think he understood when I explained it to him. "It will ruin her girlish figure," I said.

We took Pranny home, and her two weeks as a proto—nursing home patient now began. Her diet was closely regulated and cooked by me. Everything that went into her had to be monitored, and so did everything that came out, which meant that for the first time since she'd gone through therapy dog training the previous summer she was not allowed off the leash. The bag of generic dog food was discarded, since we could not be sure it wasn't tainted with melamine; not long before, thousands of pounds of kibble had been recalled after it was found to contain contaminated wheat gluten that killed at least one hundred dogs and put hundreds more into renal failure. In its place I bought the most expensive, high-end, all-natural, organic food whose ingredients and price made it clear that our dog was now eating better than we were. It was easy to justify, since however much it cost, it was going to be cheaper to buy it than to pay for regular trips to the vet if the low-end stuff continued to bother her.

This argument worked for at least a month, until the day I noticed that Pransky was limping. Close investigation revealed that she had what looked like blisters between the toes on her right paw. Back to the vet we went. This time we saw her regular doctor. He suggested that she had stepped on something that caused an infection and gave us a course of antibiotics. The paw got better. Then, a few days later, Pransky started limping again. This time the blisters were on her left foot. They were getting so familiar with us at the animal hospital that they no longer asked me my dog's name.

"Pransky's here!" the receptionist would call out, but it didn't make Pranny like the place any better.

We got the portly vet again, and when I saw him I thanked him for his previous diagnosis. No more bleeding, I told him, and joked about the ridiculously expensive food we had switched to, which Pransky was tolerating so well. Before I could extol the virtues of this new food any further, though, the doctor shut me up.

"Unfortunately, there have been a number of reports about"—and he named not only the brand but the particular honey-roasted chicken, baby carrot, Japanese eggplant, and quinoa variety we were using—"causing interdigital cysts. You'll need to wean her off the food and try something else." He taped up Pransky's sore paw and sent us home with a couple of rolls of tape. "If you're going back to the nursing home," he cautioned, "make sure her paw is covered up. You don't know what's on the floor there." The new dog food went in the trash, too. (We didn't want other dogs to get cysts between their toes.) It was like putting a match to a fifty-dollar bill.

Pransky returned to the nursing home with both legs wrapped in flesh-colored bandages that extended from her elbows over and around the bottom of her paws, which made it look like she was wearing support hose. But not to Joe. Joe, who almost never put on the prostheses that leaned up against the wall of his room, looked at Pransky's bandages, then pointed to his own. He was right, they did look similar.

"I know," I said to him, since I was pretty sure this was what he was getting at, though I couldn't be completely certain since his words had become more garbled since our first day at County. It was strange— he'd string together syllables that sounded like English but weren't, and then every so often interject a clear, discernible word. His aphasia was definitely worse, and I wondered if I was noticing it only now because we'd been away for so many weeks or if his language skills had fallen off a cliff since we'd last been there. I also wondered if he knew. I'm sure I was not alone in pretending to know what he was saying and responding in kind. Could he tell I was faking it? He was inscrutable.

What wasn't in doubt was his reaction to the dog. He reached out to her as soon as he saw her coming down the hall. But when she drew closer, it was clear that his hands were no longer working as well as they had before, either. I wondered if his diabetes had progressed or if he'd had another stroke. Not that it mattered. At a certain stage of life, I was learning, consequences were more important than causes. You had to live with the consequences.

It was a stroke. Not more than half an hour later, after Pranny and I had finished our visits on the rehabilitation wing, we saw Joe again, this time in the company of two middle-aged women and a middle-aged man, all in street clothes, who I guessed—correctly—were relatives, and it was mentioned in passing.

"Is this Pransky?" one of the women asked. I said it was.

"Dad just loves this dog," she said. "He loves all dogs, but he really loves this dog." Then she told me about the stroke, and how she thought Pransky could help with Joe's depression. As we were speaking, Joe called Pransky over and she put her front paws in his lap. It was a trick I'd taught her, so people in wheelchairs and hospital beds would not have to bend over to pet her, but she was supposed to do it only when I said the words "two paws up." Under normal circumstances, she knew, without the command, putting her paws up was completely illegal. But she also must have known that these were not normal circumstances.

"Like," Joe said, and while it wasn't clear if he meant

he liked her up there, or that her legs looked like his stumps, it was clear that, if only briefly, he had been released from the burdens of body and mind. Pransky had known how to do that.

It was a Friday afternoon, not our usual Tuesday morning, and the place seemed different. We'd been absent, and a lot of people we passed in the hall made it a point to reach down to Pransky and welcome her back and comment on her dramatic leg wraps, so there was that. The rhythm was different, too, and so was the way the light came through the windows. A raucous bingo game was under way in the activities room—raucous because Scotty would yell "What?" after every call, and then everyone else would repeat the number, but a couple would get the number wrong, which would cause Scotty to shout "What?" again, and the caller to repeat the number.

"It could drive you to drink," Clyde said, and rolled out of the room, disgusted. Pransky and I moved into Clyde's spot and played a round. We had two cards, one for each of us, and because I was sitting next to Scotty, I was helping him with his card, too.

"Bingo!" I shouted enthusiastically not more than ten minutes into the game.

"What are you saying?" Scotty said petulantly. "I have bingo? I don't have bingo! Do I have bingo?"

"Pransky has bingo," I explained. "The dog. The dog has bingo!" I showed him her card.

"Dogs can't play bingo!" Scotty said indignantly. "Dogs don't have hands!"

"True," I said. "I was playing for her."

"Oh," Scotty said, mollified. "I didn't realize."

I picked out a prize for Pransky, a small stuffed unicorn that she happily accepted and held in her mouth.

"Let's go show it off," I said, and we made our exit, heading over to the west corridor. Iris and Dottie, I knew, would be eager to see it and, even more, to see Pran. Iris had taken to calling Pransky Dottie's cousin. She was sure they were related.

Two things struck me when I peeked into Iris and Dottie's room that afternoon. The first was that they were just sitting there. Iris was in the far corner, her back to the window, her body framed by the sunlight, her eyes open, staring idly into the middle distance, wherever that was. A few feet away, Dottie faced the television, which was turned off, its black screen broadcasting her own dull stare back to her. The scene could have been a stop-action photograph—call it "Two Nonagenarians Going About Their Day in a Nursing Home"—except, of course, that there was no action to stop. They were captured in time, not just figuratively but literally as well.

The second thing was what happened when Pransky and I broke into the frame. Seeing us standing in the doorway, Iris said, "But it's not Tuesday." It was true. It was not Tuesday, it was Friday, which meant that Iris not only remembered that we typically came on Tuesdays but that she knew what day it was right then, which is to say—and this is what struck me—Iris was oriented in time.

When a person has a head injury, or dementia is suspected, one of the first questions they are asked is if they know what day it is. It's a way of assessing how out of it, or not, they are. In a hospital, one of the things that happens, even to people without memory problems or compromised brains, is that they lose track of time. Hospital staff are in and out of their rooms at all hours, the lights are often on continuously, especially in intensive care, noise is constant, and the border between night and day blurs. A nursing home is almost the complete opposite of this. There isn't a lot going on, so Monday bleeds into Tuesday which bleeds into Wednesday which bleeds into Thursday till all days are one, unending, indistinguishable day. That was why, I suspected, the staff at County made sure to hang a copy of the monthly activities calendar on everyone's closet door, with a clear line of sight from there to the bed, and why there were strategically placed whiteboards throughout the place announcing the day's events, and why it was important that bingo was on Fridays and classic movies were on Mondays. These, along with the many holidays celebrated there, became a way to saw the plank of time into distinct steps that at least gave the illusion of going somewhere. (One morning, Dan, who had taken to lying on his bed with a pillow over his eyes all day unless cajoled out of his room for a baking project or an activity that involved eating sweets, asked if I could get him "one of those picture things with numbers that they had at the dollar store," which I took to mean a calendar. A few days later he asked Carol if she could put a second wall clock in his room so he would never have to turn his head to know the hour, which probably had more to do with his being adrift in time than being anchored to it.)

"It's not Tuesday!" Iris said, and I was pleased, the

same way I'd been pleased when Dottie began to say "See you next week" when we said goodbye. They were both firmly rooted in space and time, even though they had been sitting there, stock-still, for how long?

The "how long?" question was one I thought about a lot when I tried to imagine myself as a County resident, stripped of all but a few possessions, dependent on other people for meals and care, sharing a room with a stranger, eager for affection from someone else's dog. After only a few months at County, I understood the phrase "Old age is not for sissies" better than before, if I'd actually ever understood it before. And I was getting older myself, and Pransky was getting older even faster, so that the unbending facts of my own mortality and hers lurked ever closer to the surface of my consciousness. At a different point in my life I would have considered that to be the downside of spending time in a nursing home, but spending time in a nursing home had changed me: which is to say that I did not. The unasked-for gift of being with people at the end of their lives was not dissimilar to the gift that people who have come through tragedies or accidents or life-threatening illnesses report having been given by those events, which is a simple but profound appreciation of the here and now of life itself. Everyone, everywhere, has burdens, but watching many of the residents at County bear theirs was a simple lesson in the not-so-simple virtue of fortitude—of everyday quotidian valor. Until the nursing home, I'd thought of fortitude, like its near relation, courage, as belonging, pretty much exclusively, to the young and to the strong, which may be a bias of the young and the strong; it takes time itself to truly understand that strength is more than a physical attribute.

In 1903, the Reverend William Huntington told the congregation of New York City's Grace Church that while fortitude is commonly considered a Stoic virtue, he believed that "the Stoics betrayed themselves when they sanctioned suicide as the brave man's last resort. For what kind of a courage is that," he asked, "which can be brave enough to die, but confesses itself, under some circumstances, not brave enough to live?" He continued, "As old age draws on, with its prospect of isolation by bereavement, its prospect of increasing bodily infirmity, its prospect of waning mental powers, its prospect of declining influence, the man is brave indeed who puts on a bold front. This is more than physical courage, because it includes physical courage. It is physical courage plus." The title of his sermon, delivered near the end of his life, was "The Credentials of a Good Old Age."

was pretty sure that Dottie, sitting there that day in a jaunty white cardigan sweatshirt embroidered with monarch butterflies and doing a whole lot of nothing, was not having a good old age. For one thing, she could not hear, which cut her off from almost everyone and everything around her. For another, one of her sons lived in the Sunbelt and got up north to see her only once a year, though he called every night, and the other had recently died.

Pransky and I had learned of the loss from an aide the day after it happened. Although Dottie was alone most of the time except for sharing the room with Iris, she generally managed to stay on an even keel, or at least to appear so. But that morning the aide had found her crying and keening, and Dottie had told her that her son had died during the night. The aide hoped Pransky might be able to help pull Dottie out of her funk.

"I hear that Dottie's son died," I said to Janie as she

was handing me that day's visiting list. "We'll go there first."

Janie cocked her head and looked perplexed. "That's the thing," she said. "He didn't die. It was a dream. She just dreamed that he died."

A week later, though, Dottie's son actually did die. Somehow, she had known.

So here we were, visiting out of order, on a day we were not supposed to be there, as Iris pointed out right away. "It's a gorgeous day," I said to her. "It's beautiful outside," I said to Dottie, mouthing the words as distinctly as I could.

"Hot?" she asked.

"Not at all," I said, shaking my head to make sure she understood. Weather, I'd noticed, was like a distant relation that County residents were constantly asking after. This wasn't just to make conversation. For most of their lives, as farmers and farmers' wives, they had been wedded to the weather. Now that they were living indoors for the most part, they were largely divorced from it, but not amicably. They missed it. Even when it was ugly, they missed it.

"It's warm out. Nice," I told Dottie, and as I did, an idea popped into my head that was so plain and obvious that it almost seemed radical: Pransky and I would take her outside. "Would you like to take Pransky for a walk?" I said to Dottie, slipping Pransky's leash off my wrist and wrapping it around hers. She looked at me curiously, and so did Pran. Handing over the reins to a frail, deaf, elderly woman in a wheelchair definitely broke every therapy dog handling rule while simultaneously voiding the terms of our liability insurance. If it worked—and it was up to Pransky to make it work—great—and if it didn't, all bets were off. One errant pull from Pransky and Dottie would be launched into the air, if not to sudden death. I knelt down and went eye to eye with my dog. I told her what she needed to do and what she could not, under any circumstances, even contemplate—a list that included chasing after pigeons, squirrels, lunch meat, other dogs. It was game time, and it was imperative for her to understand that even if Dottie was holding the leash, I was still calling the shots. I hoped my tone conveyed both how much trust I was placing in her, and how crucial it was that she listen to me. I might have added a preemptive "don't be a bad dog" in there, too. Then we took off down the hall, with Pransky in the lead, me giving her constant feedback ("slow," "good," "good slow," "good dog," "good slow dog"), and Dottie in between us, holding the leash with both hands like she was driving a team of horses.

"Mush, mush!" one of the residents called out when he saw us. Other people clapped.

"This is fun!" Dottie said, turning around for a second with a huge grin on her face, then turning back just in time to steer Pranny clear of a rehab patient taking her new hip out for a stroll with the physical therapist. They stopped to let our parade pass, but not before petting the dog, admiring her leg wraps, and speaking to Dottie, which is what happened when we encountered the next person in the hall and the next and the next. Everyone was amused by the sight of Dottie "walking" the dog, and everyone said so. Dottie, suddenly, was the most popular person at County, and the expression on her face made it clear that she didn't mind this at all.

It took a while, but we finally got outdoors, and when we did I took the leash from Dottie and dropped it to the ground, giving Pransky leave to explore the neighborhood. After a few unsuccessful squirrel lunges, she returned to her lead position in front of the wheelchair, even though no one was holding her leash, and trotted a few steps ahead as I guided Dottie around the courtyard.

"Beautiful, beautiful, beautiful," Dottie said as we paused by one of the flower beds. She leaned over and buried her face in the petals and took a deep breath. "Ah," she said, exhaling. Later, I took her over to Clyde's tomatoes, which were bright red and heavy on the vine, and she ran her fingers over their smooth, taut skin, marveling at their very existence.

"Thank you," Dottie said, when we returned to her room. "Let's do that again." And we did. We did it every week for more than a year, till the day came when she could no longer hold the leash and didn't want to, anyway. On that day, Pransky climbed into bed with her and they lay together, without moving, back to back.

don't know if dogs, because they live with people, not only take on the appearance of their owners but acquire human attributes as well, and I don't know if the moral calculus of animals operates within the same parameters as ours. I do know that some dogs, like some people, when called upon, exhibit great courage, and that courage always has been counted, by philosophers and theologians, among the virtues. I would like to believe that my dog would be quick to run into a burning building to rescue a stranded child, just as I'd like to believe that I would, too, but how could we know until the building was on fire? That is the mystery of courage: it lies dormant until a situation calls upon it. Fortitude is something else altogether. To me it suggested endurance, though it is possible that in finding examples of fortitude in the ways that County residents held on and carried on against the odds—in Dottie's calm acceptance of her deafness and isolation, in Clyde's flirtations and in Fran's current events club of one, to name just a few—I was simply putting a gloss on frailty and loss. Maybe spending time at County with Pranny was making me a glass-half- or even -three-quarters-full kind of person. Maybe I was becoming more like my dog.

Some weeks after Dottie started to walk Pransky with me, on a rainy day when we could not go out into the courtyard, we were on our way down the west corridor when I noticed a seriously large, haunting, black-and-white painting on the wall of one of the rooms that hadn't been there the week before. Marta, whose painting it was, had come to County after a stroke, though how long after I didn't know. She was one of those women with luminous skin who could be any age, and her eyes, set deep and wide, suggested both warmth and intelligence. In her "before" life, I found out later, she had been an artist and an art historian, and had run a university art gallery. In her "after" life, Marta sat with Carol for hours, Carol helping her coax an unwilling hand to hold an oversized paintbrush or thick crayon, praising her when the blank paper on the table in front of them began to fill up with stabs and spots of color. Marta's ability to speak had been impaired as well, and the therapists were also trying to teach her to type so she might learn another way to communicate, but it was not happening. Looking at the walls of her room, which were hung with a dozen framed, challenging, original paintings, it was obvious that even before this "after" life, Marta's preferred means of expression was visual more than verbal. Pransky and I took to stopping by her room as if it were a gallery, standing on the far side of the bed to see the whole picture, then moving to the other side to take in the details. I made it a point to tell Marta what I was seeing, knowing full well that what I was saying to her about the work was probably as unintelligible as what she was saying to me. It was a weird kind of parity.

And then someone—it could have been Carol, or Janie, or one of the local artists who stopped by to visit Marta—had the idea of having an art show at County. It would be a real one, with professional artists, curated by Marta. A call went out, artists responded, invitations were sent, the paintings were hung under Marta's watchful eye, and the night of the opening, the place was packed. It would have been easy to find sadness in the whole thing—it was there for the taking. You could have seen the exhibit, hung on the wan, pastel walls of a public nursing facility as a great comedown for an art historian who had been to every major museum and gallery in the world, a curator who had exhibited many great works herself, and an artist steeped in the smell of oils and turpentine. And while you would not have been wrong, you would not have been right, either. Writing about the painter Marie-Louise Motesiczky, "who sailed into her eighties gracefully in spite of physical pain," Diana Athill, who at the time was in her nineties, said, "She was wonderful to talk with about painting, and it explained why there was no feeling of emptiness about her. She was an object lesson on the essential luck, whatever hardships may come their way, of those born to make things." Some of that luck was Marta's, too, and with help she was able to make the best of it.

While the luck was innate, the help was not, and the help was essential. I often wondered how the staff at County did it—how the people who worked there kept their good humor, how they didn't get gloomy, disaffected, or mean. The misdeeds and cruelty of nursing home workers have been well documented, and the prospect of mistreatment is one reason people fear ending up in a place like County. But not, in fact, a place like County, because at County, the staff, almost to a person, was friendly and kind. Still, there were not enough people working there, which was a consequence of the long hours, the heavy lifting, the low wages, and County's dependence on government largesse: there was no money to bring on more staff. The economics did not work in County's favor, and because of it, the women and men who worked there had to take up the slack for the women and men who should have been working there. This meant longer hours, more shifts, more residents to dress and bathe, more medicines to dispense, more messes to clean up, more beds to make, more call buttons to answer, at any hour, for any reason. (One reason was

Pransky, who sometimes, inadvertently and unwittingly, would sit on a call button when she was invited into a resident's bed.) It was, by any measure, hard physical labor, most of it crucial yet unseen and unacknowledged, and while there may have been grousing in the staff room, I never heard it in the hall or in anyone's room, even for good cause. Mrs. Carter, for instance, kept forgetting she'd just been to the bathroom, so almost as soon as she'd leave it she'd ring for the aide, and the aide would arrive, and tell her that she'd just been to the bathroom, and they'd have a back-and-forth about it ("No, I haven't." "Yes, you have." "Well, I have to go again."); the aide would leave, and ten minutes later she'd be summoned again. And Mr. Carter, sometimes, could not decide if he wanted to wear his brown belt or his black belt and would ask whoever was walking by to switch them for him, black to brown to black to brown. Though the east corridor was locked, people would sometimes wander out anyway, and their ankle alarms would sound, and they'd have to be escorted back. "Come on, now, darling," one of the aides or nurses would say, draping an arm over the wanderer's shoulder and guiding him back. "Let's go, hon." They said these words—"darling," "sweetheart," "honey"—not because they didn't know a person's name but because they knew these people and liked them. It wasn't unusual to see laundry workers out in the courtyard tossing plastic horseshoes with residents, or housekeepers sitting side by side with them in the activities room, making Christmas ornaments. Mixing socially with the residents was part of everyone's job description, and it added a measure of levity and humanity all around. Having dogs present helped, too. Pransky gave the housekeepers a chance to put down their mops and pails; she gave the nurses a chance to play; she gave the physical therapists the opportunity to talk about their own dogs; she gave the maintenance men an excuse to stop mowing and run their hands through her soft hair. Janie often said that the staff was as much in need of dog therapy as the residents were, and Pransky was happy to oblige.

Still, sometimes I worried about her. She would leave the nursing home each week, climb into the backseat of the car, stretch out, and fall into a deep sleep. Then she'd go home and curl up in her bed and sleep some more. When we were at the nursing home it seemed like she was getting as much out of the encounters with residents and staff as they were. Her tail wagged, she often appeared to be smiling, and who wouldn't bask in all that affection? But all that affection took something out of her, too. Part of it was having to be on her best behavior all the time, and part was having to pay close attention to my words and gestures, but another part was that she couldn't choose who got to pat her head, and because she couldn't choose who, she also couldn't choose the how and where—how hard they touched her, or where they touched her. Somehow, intuitively, she understood that it was part of the job to accommodate everyone's needs, whether the effect was pleasant or not. Much of the time her joyfulness made her pleasure transparent, but when it wasn't pleasant—when the man who periodically pulled her tail held on to it too long, or when the woman with mild cognitive impairment forgot about Pransky's sensitive ears and rubbed them vigorously, Pransky didn't react. Odd that it was a dog who demonstrated for me why fortitude, as the Reverend Huntington told the people of Grace Church, was long considered to be a Stoic virtue, since Stoicism, at its core, was about self-control.

Eventually, this was a lesson I learned from Lizzie and her mother, though from her mother much later, since I didn't meet her until, as Diana Athill titled her memoir, "somewhere near the end." Athill, who had been a celebrated book editor in England, had a good fifty years on

Lizzie, who, in any case, looked even younger than she was, despite a disability that left her able to do little but recline most of the day in the west lounge in a plush chair that was pointed in the direction of the TV. "Puppy," Lizzie would say when she saw Pransky, and reach out with a crabbed hand and rest it on Pranny's head. It was the same every week, to the point where I think both Pransky and I expected it to be the same every week— the single word, the deliberate movement of her arm till it was extended far enough for Pransky to slip her head under Lizzie's hand, which rested there as if she were giving a benediction. But one day the chair was empty, and only Thomas was watching the television, and when I asked him where Lizzie was, he said he didn't know. Then we left him and turned the corner, and there was Lizzie, in her nightgown, being pushed in an oversized wheelchair in the direction of the shower. Apparently it was one of those days when enough people called in sick that the whole schedule was thrown into turmoil, so here was Lizzie, at ten-thirty, not yet washed and dressed.

Lizzie saw us just as we saw her. She smiled as best she could, and we went over to her, me expecting her to say "puppy," the way she always said "puppy." "Good morning, Lizzie," I said. And then to Pransky I said, "Say 'good morning' to Lizzie," by which I meant, essentially, "present yourself for petting." Before she could do this, Lizzie herself said, "Good morning, Pransky," which was two more words than she'd ever spoken in my presence, and three words I'd never heard her say, and it was oddly thrilling to hear them. If I needed more evidence that Pransky's particular brand of therapy was working, this was it. At the time I did not know what was wrong with Lizzie—I was still thinking she'd had a stroke. With ever-greater numbers of young people having strokes, Lizzie was, weirdly, from the right demographic.

As I learned later, Lizzie was, even more weirdly, from the right demographic for the rare disease that she did have, something called spinocerebellar ataxia, which was a genetic, neurodegenerative affliction that caused the cerebellum—the part of the brain that, among other things, is responsible for motor control—to atrophy. When I learned this, I also learned a few other things: that there are many kinds of ataxias, and they strike at different ages, causing different disabilities: vertigo; rapid, uncontrollable eye movements; lack of coordination; hand tremors; head tremors; seizures; loss of normal motor functions and muscle wasting; macular degeneration. "Generally, a person with ataxia retains full mental capacity," Wikipedia told me, "but may progressively lose physical control." Was it wrong to wish that this general situation did not apply specifically to Lizzie? Were those words, "Good morning, Pransky," proof that it did? How could there be a more poignant demonstration of fortitude than this?

A week later, Lizzie was not in her usual spot, but this time Carol said it was because she was not doing well and was in her room and would welcome a visit. Lizzie's room was the last one on the west wing, so we walked down there and went in, and there was Lizzie's mother, sitting in a chair, reading a book and talking to her daughter, who was in the bed. They were having a conversation, and though it was not one I completely understood, her mother obviously did. Lizzie's eyes lit up when we walked in, and Pransky did the "two-paws up" trick, and Lizzie reached out and stroked the dog. They stayed that way for a couple of minutes, till an aide came in to try to make Lizzie, who was having trouble regulating her temperature, more comfortable. There was something reassuring and normal about having Lizzie's mother in the room. A mother might not be able to do anything to stop the destructive path of a genetic disease, but she could put a cool washcloth on a hot forehead, which is what Lizzie's mother was doing when Pransky and I left them.

Certain, then, that this was a fever, I expected to see Lizzie back in her blue corduroy recliner when Pransky and I walked into the dayroom the next week, but again it was empty. Down the hall I could see that someone was sitting in a chair outside Lizzie's room, and when we got closer, I saw that it was Lizzie's mother, and she was talking calmly on a cell phone, with no sense of urgency. I guessed that she was on the phone in the hall because Lizzie was sleeping and she didn't want to wake her, but when she hung up and I asked if Lizzie was awake and wanted a visit, or was asleep and should we come back, she said, cryptically, that Lizzie was "permanently" asleep. I asked if Pransky and I should go in anyway, and she opened the door for us. Inside, Lizzie was lying in bed, eyes closed, breathing easily; her permanent sleep looked surprisingly like everyone else's regular sleep. I had seen people in comas before, and Lizzie somehow seemed calmer and more present. She was tucked in, with her arms on the outside of the blanket, her head propped on the pillow. The only evidence that this sleep was a different sort of sleep was that an eight-by-ten framed photograph of a young man in his twenties rested on her lap. Who was he, I wondered. Her brother, I decided, who lived far away and couldn't get here in time, even though I had no idea if she had a brother or, if she did, where he lived. But it could have been a photograph of her father from way back. No father was around, so maybe he'd died long ago, at the age of the man in the photo. The most obvious explanation, and the one that turned out to be true, did not even cross my mind: the young man in the photograph was her son.

Even though Lizzie appeared to be asleep, as we approached I talked to her as if she were awake, telling her that Pransky had come to visit. When we reached the bed, Pranny leaned her front paws on top of the covers, and I put my right hand over the back of Lizzie's left hand and lifted it and brought it to the dog. Holding her hand like this, we stroked Pransky's fur. Lizzie's hand was a deadweight in mine. If I let go of it, it would flop down with a thud. It was calm in the room. Lizzie's face was peaceful. It showed no pain and no sentience. She was alive, whatever that meant. Tired herself, Pransky rested her head on Lizzie's thigh and submitted to this strange sort of petting, my hand moving Lizzie's hand on the last full day of her life. She was forty-two years old.

There are lots of awards for courage—for high-risk rescues, for intervening to stop an injustice, for battlefield bravery. There are even awards for courageous dogs, including dogs of war. Courage of all sorts is crucial to society because it demonstrates a selflessness that is necessary for social cohesion. By celebrating courage publicly, the message is clear: we are all in this together. Courage begets courage.

There are no awards for fortitude. It is rare that a medal is pinned on someone for pain and suffering, or for hanging on for the long haul despite obstacles, sadness, grief, and come-what-may. There was no award for Lizzie, for twenty years of entrapment in a twisted body, and none for the mother for standing by her. There was no award for Dottie, and none for Iris or Dan or any other resident of County or the people who cared for them. According to the Catechism of the Catholic Church, "the virtue of fortitude enables one to conquer fear, even fear of death, and to face trials and persecutions." What this suggested, and what I believed I saw at County, and what I hoped was true, was that fortitude was not a virtue that one consciously practiced but rather one that accrued. And this: the reward for getting through life is getting life itself.

5.

Hope

Hope, as most English majors will remember, is "the thing with feathers," and though I had not been an English major myself, these were the words that came to me when I entered Martha's room on the east wing one day and found her staring out the window at a bird feeder planted on a pole not two feet away on the other side of the glass. The feeder was empty but drawing the interest of a couple of goldfinches searching for a stray seed or two. Martha might have been looking at the birds, or she might have been looking past them, or she might have been looking at something only she could see. Most of the time she seemed lost in her own world, sitting opposite her portable television, which was always on, and always tuned to one game show or another. We'd walk by and she'd be parked there with a cup of coffee cooling on a folding metal table in front of her, slightly hunched, a quizzical expression on her face that could have been mistaken for a smile. We'd walk back, and it was the same. When birds flew across her peripheral vision, though, they got her attention, and she'd turn away from the TV. A well-thumbed *Peterson's Field Guide to Birds of North America* had been strategically placed on the windowsill by one of her many daughters, who hoped Martha would be inclined to consult it. (She wasn't.) On this day, it was joined there by a single, plump, unblemished red tomato.

"What's your dog's name?" she asked, though by then she should have known, having asked the same question every week for nearly a year—"should" being a relative term, and one that did not apply to people whose memory was shot.

"Pransky," I said.

"Fancy?" she asked.

"Pransky," I said.

"Frisky?" she asked.

"Pranny," I said.

"Oh, Franny," she said.

"Yes," I said. "Franny."

"I had a dog once," she said.

"The white one?" I asked, though I knew the dog was white, and looked like a wolf, and could be as ferocious as she was sweet.

"We called her a wolf dog," she said.

"Was this the dog named Snowflake?" I asked.

"Yes, we called her Snowflake," she said, neither surprised to find out that I knew her dog's name nor interested in learning how I did.

I pointed to a photo on her closet door. "Is this the dog you mean?"

She said it was. She always said it was. We were on script; we'd had this conversation, or some near variant of it every week, for months. Not that Martha knew; her long-term memory was pretty good, but like many people with dementia, she lived almost exclusively in the present—the present being this very minute. Five minutes ago was often out of reach, and so was seven days ago. Week to week, Martha never remembered that she'd met us, or that she'd told me about her dog, or her eight children, or her seven siblings. From the outside looking in, it seemed an awful place to be, idling in a never-ending now, able only to go a short distance, and always in reverse. Martha, though, seemed content. If there was any blessing in dementia—and I didn't actually believe for a moment that there was—it was this erosion of self-awareness.

"That's a nice-looking tomato," I said, eyeing the Big Boy on the windowsill.

"Nothing like a ripe tomato," Martha said, with a faraway sound in her voice.

"Where did it come from?" I asked.

"Someone grew it," she said.

I supposed it was Clyde, and asked her, but she said she didn't know his name. "He said he'd give me another one when it's ripe, but I'm not going to eat this one till I can share it with someone." Martha said this more than once. I couldn't tell if this was because sharing was meaningful to her—that it recalled long-ago summer days in the fields she used to roam with her sisters and brothers—or if she had forgotten she had just said it, or both, and I knew it didn't matter, and not just because

Martha wouldn't remember this conversation, or me, or Pranny, whom she was petting as we talked. It didn't matter, because that tomato made her happy. It gave her leave to look backward and remember, even if memory was only a feeling, and it enabled her to look forward with anticipation. As static as her life appeared to me, in some crucial way that was largely imperceptible to others, it wasn't.

"Have any birds been to the feeder lately?" I asked Martha, who lit up.

"Yes!" she said, excited, as if she'd been waiting for me, or anyone, to ask.

"What kind?" I asked.

"It was blue," she said. "It was wearing a plaid skirt."

"A blue jay?" I asked

She looked at me like I was a genius. "Yes!" she said. "A blue jay. I saw a blue jay. It was beautiful." Her words—her excitement and enthusiasm—arrested me: here was a woman who had walked the earth for nearly a hundred years, and she could still be amazed by a bird that most of us barely see because it is so common, or see mainly as a nuisance. It was a little thing, but for me, at least, it had feathers.

Where do you find hope in a nursing home? Or, rather, where do you find hope without trivializing it? At first glance—the glance you give when you're driving by, and the glance you give, hands over eyes, when you feel you have no choice but to send someone you love there, or when you are the future resident in question—the answer seems simple: you don't. Dante inscribed the words "Abandon Hope All Who Enter Here" above the gates of hell, and those words might seem equally appropriate hung above the doors of a place where the old and sick are sent when there is nowhere else to go. Which raises another question altogether: Can there be hope in the presence of death?

The early theologians, especially the early Catholic theologians, answered this question by elevating hope to a virtue. For most of us living in the twenty-first century, this may seem strange. For us, hope is primarily about wishing, not about doing or being: I hope I get an A on that exam; I hope she gets better; I hope you get that promotion at work. Yet wishing for things, even good things, like someone's improved health, hardly seems virtuous. Wishing is ephemeral, pie-in-the-sky, out of our control. Where is the virtue in that?

Weirdly, it was exactly in a place like the county nursing home that Augustine or Aquinas or the early church fathers might have expected the virtue of hope to manifest itself, because for them, hope was intimately entwined with death and what came after: eternal life in the Kingdom of God. Hope, in other words, was about belief, it was about the afterlife, and it was about living and acting in this world in ways that would lead to the next.

While it was possible that the residents of County were waiting out their days, hoping for eternal life and its heavenly band of angels, I didn't see it. What I saw, instead, were Clyde's tomatoes.

Somehow, early in the spring, Clyde obtained a flat of six small tomato plants, which he immediately put in the ground. The problem was that County was located so far north that the growing season was around three months, and the last day for frost was typically at the end of May. Gardeners are hopeful people, so when Clyde planted that first flat in mid-April, on a mild day when the crocuses had come and gone, he wasn't expecting the temperatures to dip again below freezing; history can't compete with sunshine and a warm breeze, but history usually wins. Pransky and I came upon Clyde with his second flat of tomatoes on May twenty-fifth. "Good morning, darling," he said to Pransky, having figured out that she was more susceptible to his charms than I. He was holding a trowel in one hand and scratching the earth; the tomato plants and a watering can were nearby. Grumbling about the weather and the quality of the soil like gardeners everywhere, he dug a hole, put some water in it, and vigorously tore a single seedling from the block of plants. The ripping sound caused Pransky to startle. "It's all right, girl," Clyde said kindly, and moved on to the second plant. Pransky caught sight of a chipmunk, raced over in its direction, then stood under the tree it climbed, her tail cocked, waiting expectantly.

"Hey!" Clyde said. "Hey, sweetheart!" Pransky trotted obediently back over to him. He was that kind of guy.

Less than a month later, Clyde's tomato plants were two feet tall and pregnant. The key, Clyde said, was "fertilizing the hell out of them with Miracle-Gro." He thought he'd have ripe fruit in a month, which was some kind of record. He also mentioned that he'd had pneumonia and probably would not be able to move back into his trailer home in Florida anytime soon. He didn't sound too disappointed when he said this. He was focused on his plants.

The wheelchair-height raised beds were scattered throughout the courtyard and tended by residents, staff, and master gardeners from all over. Even those who did not enjoy digging in the dirt or, who were no longer able, could enjoy the fruits of someone else's labor, if only by looking out the window. The flower beds were lush, and the vegetable beds were prolific. Putting seeds or seedlings in the ground, tending them, and watching them grow is, of course, the standard metaphor—which is to say the cliché—for hope. Things (people, puppies, cucumbers, blue jays) come into this world, things die, and other things come into this world: What is more hopeful than that? Even if Clyde did not look at his tomato plants and think, consciously, "Here is the cycle of life," growing tomatoes gave him a stake in the future, which is how hope prospers.

This was a useful thought to hold on to when Clyde began to fade. It was after the last tomatoes had been savored, and another winter had passed, and it seemed to happen suddenly. One day Clyde was going to bingo and flirting and wanting to talk about the time he drove his truck all the way from Connecticut to Alaska and back, and then, all of a sudden, he was showing up at the door of the office Janie shared with Carol and the others on the activities staff saying that he did not know where he was. This was after more than a dozen years of living in the same place and walking the same three hallways that together made the nursing home's simple horseshoe foot-print. There might have been signs, like the time at the Episcopal church service when the pastor asked who the congregation should pray for and Clyde said "me," but they were only signs in retrospect. One day he started getting lost in a building where he knew everyone and everyone knew him. Escorted back to his room, he would argue like a little kid that it was not his, despite his name written in black marker on the white compression socks in the top drawer of the cupboard, despite the photo-graph of his beloved niece on the wall. Soon he stopped leaving that room at all. And not long after that, he stopped getting out of bed. That's where he was the morning Pransky and I were visiting with Leslie, who lived opposite, when he let out a series of high-pitched yelps that sounded like an animal being tortured. *"Help! Help! Help! Help!"* he then began to shout desperately. Leslie was about to press her call button, but Clyde's shouts were more effective: two aides came running down the hall and rushed into Clyde's room and shut the door. Even with it closed, though, we could hear him crying.

A week later, walking down the hall, I noticed that the door to Clyde's room was open, and though the lights were off and the shades were drawn, Pransky and I went in. Clyde was in bed with the sheets pulled up to his shoulders. He seemed to be naked, but I couldn't be sure. His dentures were out, and, seeing the dog, he smiled a weak, toothless smile. He started to talk to her, and Pransky went right over and rested her chin on his pillow, as if she wanted to be so close as not to miss a word. They stayed like this, nose-to-nose, for quite a while, even after he shut his eyes and stopped talking. I imagined that when she breathed, he felt it. He seemed to be at peace.

t didn't take long for people to start telling Clyde stories. He was the guy people liked to complain about
when he was alive, and then were surprised to find they
missed when he was gone. He had remained a character
in a place where illness and old age often dulled personalities like steel on glass, and that turned out to matter
more than his grumbling or his overfondness for the
ladies. And he had been at County for so long that he had
become a fixture akin to something attached to the wall
with wood screws and molly bolts. The longer he lived at
County, the longer he seemed destined to live there. It
didn't make sense mathematically, but emotionally it did.

I, too, missed Clyde, which was reassuring. Most of
the time, death blew over me like a chill wind that dis-
sipated almost as soon as I felt it. I had always thought of
myself as a fairly compassionate person, but I started to
have my doubts. I was sorry when someone died, and
sad, but not in an overwhelming or deep or soulful way.
Pransky and I would arrive at the nursing home at ten
a.m. and I'd check the list of residents we were supposed
to visit that day, and ask Janie for any updates. "Mrs.
So-and-so on West died last Thursday," she might say, or,

"We had two deaths over the weekend," although that was unusual. Most weeks, no one died. Death hovered at the nursing home but rarely landed. When it did, and Janie let me know, I'd say, "Oh, that's a shame," or, "That's too bad, I liked Mrs. So-and-so," as if her passing were somehow about me.

"The death of any one man diminishes me," the poet John Donne wrote, and in the scheme of things, of course, he was right: the death of one person, whose tenure on this earth brought forth something new and unanticipated, diminishes "the all" of us. But in the context in which I found myself, the death of any one person, especially if it was not accompanied by pain and suffering, seemed strangely affirming. When young people die it is always, without exception, tragic. When very old people die, especially people with whom you don't have a long, complicated, intimate history, it brings to mind the necessary wisdom of Ecclesiastes (or The Byrds or Bob Dylan, depending on your orientation) about there being a time for everything, birth and death included. If we are lucky, we get to live very long and healthy lives. If we are even luckier, we will be astonished by the sight of blue jays all the way through.

It was different after Fran died, and now after Clyde.

Fran's body may have been inflexible and twisted, it may have made her an invalid with rare exceptions, but her mind was so nimble and curious that it defied chronology: she was simply too young to die, which was tragic. It was possible that death released her from a life of pain, and that it was welcomed, but it was equally possible that calling death a release was one those stories that we tell ourselves to feel better when the alternative is feeling worse. Fran's death was the one chill breeze that stayed, and not just with me, but with Pransky, too. We were the punch line for a cosmic physics joke: both Pransky and I felt Fran's absence. Every trace of her was gone from County, and someone else was in her bed, and that nothingness became the thing that was her. Pransky, who used to turn in anticipation toward Fran's door as we approached from the hall, now walked by without a glance or the subtlest sideward movement. There was nothing in that room that drew her in, and no one in that room who was anything to her. Even when that new person's name was on our visiting list, it took weeks before we ventured in—me because it felt strangely disloyal, as if I was declaring that the people in the beds were interchangeable, and Pransky because the place was a void. When Fran lived there, Pranny knew it was Fran's room.

Once Fran's clothes were emptied from the bureau and her pictures were removed from the wall, all Pransky knew was that it wasn't.

Clyde's death was different, too. Clyde was different. He was always scheming about leaving the nursing home, not in a box, which is how he did finally manage it, but in a red convertible, on the arm of a gorgeous woman. Never mind that he wore Coke-bottle glasses and had trouble seeing and walking, never mind that his frame had shrunk and his spine was curved, never mind that he had mottled skin and his teeth were gone. Clyde was a dreamer. To him, the county nursing home might as well have been the county jail, and he was convinced that through his cunning and good looks he would escape, and half the time he could convince you it was true. Why is hope a virtue? Because it does not capitulate. Because it stands up to the negative, to the void, and does not back down. Because it creates possibility in the world. Hope makes the expansion of the universe more than a physical fact. It is a defiant act of creativity and of imagination. That was Clyde, through and through. Hope is the thing with feathers because it lets the earthbound take flight.

Still, the finality of death was jarring. Always. No more Fran. No more Clyde. No more Joe. They were . . .

gone. Clyde once told me about a courtyard chipmunk that would crawl onto his shoulder and eat peanuts from his shirt pocket, "but then he disappeared." Then Clyde disappeared, leaving only the husks of his story, soon to scatter and be forgotten. Did Pransky understand that Clyde had died? Or Joe, or Fran? Did it matter? Certainly she knew they were gone, but it was not clear if the duration of their absence meant anything to her. When someone died our routine changed, which made an impression. But then new routines would supplant old ones, and then others would supplant those. Pransky had loved climbing into bed with Fran and loved going for walks with Dottie, but when these were no longer in the offing there were other beds and other friends, though never anyone else to squire up and down the corridors and around the courtyard garden, never anyone to say the things Clyde would say when his mouth was next to her ear and he was whispering. I tried to emulate my dog— to channel her easy way of letting go and moving on, if that's what it was—and I think most of the time I did. And yet. And yet an unconscious empathy—or maybe it was fear—led me sometimes to imagine what it must have been like to be the person in the bed, and it left me wondering this: If you have been able to live the life

you've wanted and hoped to live, a life without regrets (if
such a thing is possible), and if you've done the things
you've wanted to do, been the sort of person you've
wanted to be, left behind whatever legacy for those
behind you you'd hope to leave, and so on, do you face
death with equanimity, as we've been led to think such a
life would allow us, or with utter grief because you know
how good it's been, and death is like all your regrets
saved up for one big blowout? I didn't know, and hoped
not to know for a long time, but the question came back,
time and time again, and the people who might have
answered it couldn't.

I f hope was the thing with feathers, at County it was also
the thing with pink curlers, conditioner, and a boar's-
hair brush—Jasmine's beauty shop. Located in an alcove
between the nursing home's administrative offices and
one of its three nurses' stations, the beauty shop was pre-
sided over by a middle-aged woman named Jasmine,
with long black hair, stylish red glasses, and a merry
aura. As County's resident beautician, Jasmine had been
at the nursing home for twenty-one years, longer, even,
than Clyde, longer than Janie. In that time, she had

developed a way with thinning white and lank gray hair. Women would roll into her shop, with its single sink-and-dryer setup, and she'd wash, cut, set, and dry their hair no differently than if they'd still been able to go to one of the salons in town. They'd chat and gossip. Secrets were revealed, jokes made. It was a happy place that Jasmine made even happier with playful decorations: one time she outfitted the room to look like a bridal shop; on Valentine's Day she wrapped it in hearts and red crepe paper.

No one had to have her hair done. No one had to look better than she did after the standard morning shampoo in the shower. Yet Jasmine's appointment book was always full. Barbara Burch was a regular, Iris was a regular, Dottie was a regular, everyone seemed to be a regular—age and infirmity, apparently, did not dull the desire to get, in Jasmine's words, "dolled up." I suppose someone could argue that wanting to get dolled up near the end of life was a sign that women were still bound by the shackles of social convention, but that would be a weak, purely theoretical argument. Standing at the threshold of Jasmine's domain with Pransky, who was not allowed by State Health Department rules to go any farther, I'd watch as the affectless perked up under Jasmine's sway, or the passive suddenly articulated definite ideas about how they'd like to look. If this was what a lifetime of wanting to be attractive wrought, more power to it. Hope lurked under the hood of Jasmine's dryer. Hope radiated from the end of her curling iron. The simple maxim was this: people without hope for today, let alone for tomorrow, did not get their hair done.

Grace caught sight of Pransky as she was sitting in front of the beauty shop mirror while Jasmine brushed out her long, thick silver mane. She called out, loud enough to cause us to stop. She wanted to see the dog. Pransky sat down. I leaned against the door frame. Jasmine turned the chair around so Grace could gaze at Pransky while she worked. Often, just the sight of the dog would make people happy, or at least brighten their mood. Calling this therapy seemed grandiose, but drugs were sometimes given to achieve the same effect, and what was that called? Grace was getting an unadulterated dose of Pransky.

"Come to my room later," she said in a voice that could be described only as old-fashioned. "I have something for you."

Grace's room was on the east wing. Her "something" was a hot-dog-in-a-bun-shaped dog biscuit, which she shook out of a long plastic cylinder and fed to Pransky, who was doing her "two-paws up" trick on the edge of Grace's bed. Pransky finished the first treat, and Grace absently fed her another while she told me about the farm she'd grown up on.

"Illegal," I hissed at my dog, who ignored me and inched herself forward on the mattress. "Down. Enough."

"I think she should only have two," I said to Grace, who interpreted this as "only two more." Pransky ate the biscuits daintily, as if they were the hors d'oeuvres they were meant to resemble, then lay down on the floor and went to sleep.

"You're not being a very good guest," I told her. She opened her eyes for a second, thumped her tail, then closed her eyes again. We were done.

Grace's farm was still in the family, she told me, but farming was not. "No one goes there except sometimes to camp," she said, and shrugged, suggesting that this was just the way of the world. All the farm animals were gone except for a big Belgian draft horse named Cadillac Kate, a glorious creature so animate in Grace's mind that she believed the horse was still alive and bunking in the old barn on the property, pasturing on the land by day.

"I love driving the horses, especially Kate," she said, forgetting, it seemed, where she was. "One time I was driving her in the Fourth of July parade and someone rolled a firecracker under us and she reared up and I was sure I'd be thrown, but a man jumped out from the crowd and grabbed her harness and pulled her down. It was something to see. She is a very big girl. I love that horse."

Farm stories—everyone seemed to have them, and Pransky seemed to trigger them. One day in the fall of our first year at County, Pransky and I walked into Martha's room, and sitting catercorner to her was another elderly woman who introduced herself as Martha's sister, Dora. Martha's older sister, she added. Dora had white curly hair, where Martha's was gray and straight; she wore a skirt, while Martha had on her usual faded denim pants; and her eyes were focused and direct, unlike Martha's, which had a permanent farawayness to them. Born in 1913, Dora was then ninety-seven. She had driven over (in her car, by herself) for a visit, before heading down to Florida where she had friends. For Dora, unlike Martha, the present was as fully accessible as the past, though it was the past that I wanted to ask her about: the first cars on the road, the two World Wars, the first commercial airplanes, the Great Depression. She remembered something about them all. "The Depression wasn't too bad," she said, "since we grew our own food. And the thing was, Prohibition was good for us. My father had a still out in the woods, and planes would land in our field and he'd sell them the whiskey and they'd take it back to New York City."

I wasn't sure about my dog, but I was a sponge for stories like Dora's. Across the street, at the college, young people were studying twentieth-century history from a book. Over here at the nursing home, no one called it history, they called it life—their life. Iris, for example, was born the same year Archduke Ferdinand was assassinated, setting off the cascade of geopolitical dominoes that led to World War I. Electricity as we know it had been invented before that, but Iris grew up in a house without it, heated by two woodstoves and lit by kerosene lanterns. It took a horse and buggy half a day to get from her parents' farm to her grandmother's, one town away. Eventually they had a telephone, and it was on a party line. Most of us were born into modernity; Dora and Iris had watched it unfold.

"Nowadays people meet on the Internet," Iris said

dismissively. "They don't even know each other. That's why the divorce rate is so high." She had met her husband at a dance and married him when she was eighteen. He died when she was fifty-eight. Theirs was a long marriage by almost any measure—but now, at ninety-six, she'd been widowed longer. I was impressed that she knew about Internet dating, but that was because she was still in the habit of reading a newspaper every day. "Things happen too fast now," she said. "It's all superficial and shallow."

"Lots of cultural critics have been saying the same thing," I said, which did not seem to interest her in the least. Cultural critics? What did that even mean to an elderly woman in a nursing home?

"I think it's all stupid," she declared, and that was that. Old age and her own failing body had conspired to convince Iris that everything else in the world was going to hell, too, and there was no talking her out of it. Politicians were corrupt, cities were dangerous, men were dangerous, young people were discourteous (and when you were on the cusp of one hundred, pretty much everyone was a young person), medicine offered false promises, same-sex marriage was evil, the food at County should not be called food, and on and on. The only vacation from pessimism seemed to come from my visits with Pransky, which gave Dottie such joy that it carried away Iris, too.

ris, like Grace, Dottie, and Martha, had grown up on a farm, but none of her children lived on one, which was the case for almost everyone at County, especially the women. Their personal stories mirrored the American story, especially the rural American economic story, which started out on the land but moved off it once work for wages got factored in and wants supplanted needs. Once she was married, Iris left the farm for good, too, raising her family in town while her husband worked in a factory. In the mornings she'd get up early and make doughnuts that he'd take with him and sell to the other workers to supplement their income. She looked after other people's children. She grew peonies. She didn't learn to drive until she was nearly sixty and she had little choice because her husband had died. Education meant a high school diploma—college was for someone else. But then her children grew up, and if they didn't continue their education, their own children did. At County it was not unusual to find someone who had left school in the eighth grade and who now had grandchildren, or great-grandchildren, in graduate school. Clyde had been fond of showing off a picture of his niece, who, he bragged, "went to college for eight years and got straight As" and was a lawyer in Boston. Stella's walls were covered with postcards from her granddaughter's travels: the granddaughter was taking a year off after college—"taking a year off" being a concept as removed from Stella's experience as college itself.

The men's lives followed similar patterns. Thomas's eighty Holsteins were long gone. Dan had sold his dairy farm to a man who raised beef cattle for a couple of years before selling the land, in turn, to someone who made his money putting up subdivisions with names like Angus Acres. Louie Brant was an exception, I learned, when he called Pransky and me into his room one morning, despite the sign on his door suggesting that entering was a health risk. Louie had hung on to his land and his cows and, despite his advanced age and a body that had clearly seen better days, was still running his farm along with his children, who were committed to keeping it going. "Big farms are doomed to fail," he told me, kicking off an impromptu lesson in farm economics—punctuated by baby talk to Pransky—that I would have expected from a college-educated locavore rather than a rough-hewn eighty-six-year-old missing all but his incisors. "They are doomed to fail because they have to borrow so much money to support themselves and then they flood the market with their product and the price goes down and then they can't make enough money to support themselves." On his small farm, history was making a full circle, but even Louie was not optimistic that the farm would last through another revolution. "It's all about money," he said.

Louie was exceptional in another way, too: he went home. One week he was there, with the "consult with the nurse before entering" sign on his door, and the next week the sign had been removed and someone else's quilt was on the bed. Attrition being what it was at County— and why—I assumed the worst. Janie set me straight. "It does happen sometimes," she said. I wondered if it happened to Mr. Brant because his farm and his farm family were still intact. He had something to look forward to and he was needed—no one knew more about that acreage and those animals than he did—and he was able enough.

When Grace was missing the next week, I didn't

assume she'd gone home, wherever that was now, but I didn't think that she'd died, either. She was too healthy—too alive—for that. She was the Cadillac Kate of the east wing. She must be working with the physical therapist, I told Pransky, who was very fond of Grace's special treats. I was certain that we'd run into her somewhere on our circuit. Then someone mentioned in passing that Grace was over at the hospital, and since County residents went to the hospital all the time for doctor visits and X-rays and CAT scans, Grace's absence made sense. County was a single-story building with few nooks and crannies—of course we hadn't seen Grace.

The week after we'd met her at the beauty shop, Grace had started a new tradition: she would meet us in the foyer, and while I was disinfecting my hands at the sanitizer dispenser there, she would entertain Pransky with food. When she ran out of dog biscuits, she saved parts of dinner or lunch for her. The therapy dog rules said nothing about forbidding a dog a gift of food, so I just pretended I didn't see what was going on, though sometimes Grace would ask me to pick apart the food from the napkin it was wrapped in.

When Grace did not greet us the next week, either, I

asked around and learned that she had been admitted to the hospital. No one was saying why she was there, or what was wrong, and I knew enough not to ask. But I was sure she'd be out of the hospital in no time. Grace appeared to be one of the more robust residents, perfectly able to get herself around the facility, conversant, thoughtful, someone who could plan enough ahead to have dog treats to distribute on Tuesdays.

"She's probably saving you something yummy right now," I told Pranny.

I wasn't worried. Intentionally or not, I had internalized a matrix, which was completely made up, to understand where I thought a person fell on the timeline of mortality: whether she was frail or not, whether she was confused or lucid. If she was frail and confused, the outlook was not promising. If she was robust and lucid, the outlook was better. Since Grace was not frail, and she seemed lucid most of the time, I assumed she'd be around for a long time. This was not scorekeeping, and it wasn't scientific. Rather, it was a way for me, in a place where people would die eventually, to be prepared.

Most of the time, the matrix served me. There was a woman Pransky and I had been visiting who greeted us warmly and played with the dog, and because she was on the younger side of residents at the nursing home, and lively, she seemed destined either for an extended stay at County, or possibly, like Louie, for a return home. Then she started losing weight, and while the loss was incremental, it was also cumulative and dramatic, so that after a few weeks her clothes hung off her bones and her eyes had retreated into their sockets, and when we came upon her sitting in the hallway one day, she began to cry. "That dog doesn't like me!" she said.

"That's not true," I countered. "Of course she likes you."

"No," she insisted, "your dog does not like me."

I told her I didn't see how that could be true. What did seem true to me, what I suddenly understood, was that she was not going to live much longer. It wasn't what she looked like, per se, it was her flat affect, which seemed as drained of hope as her cheeks were drained of color. A week later, a week she'd spent confined to bed, her face had become doughy and bloated, as if it was a death mask she was wearing as a kind of annunciation. The news of her passing the following week came as no surprise to me. It registered, but mostly as confirmation of something I already knew, not as something out of the ordinary. Death was an infection that ran its course, vanquishing its host along the way.

Grace came back to the nursing home after two weeks in the hospital. She was in her old room, Janie told me, and her family was there, too, and they'd specifically requested a visit from Pransky. That was all I knew, and because Grace had seemed so strong before she went to the hospital, I assumed she'd be sitting up, chatting, and eager for some dog time. Instead, we found her lying in her bed in a fetal position, eyes closed, her beautiful hair disheveled and soaked in sweat, moaning, writhing, insensible. I thought I had seen death before, and people dying, but I had never seen anything like this. Grace's body was gray and moving so rapidly it looked gelatinous. The word that came to mind was "primordial." Grace seemed to be returning to a time before time.

The bed was raised a good three feet off the ground, and its rails were up, so Pransky could see nothing. Still, she must have sensed it, though—"it" being death and dying—or smelled it lurking in that room. We had only been at County for a few months then, and it was Pransky's first encounter with a person who was less in this world than out of it. I wasn't sure how she would react: Would she notice, would she shy away, would she do what a lot of people do and pretend it wasn't happening? I pointed to the chair next to the bed and Pransky climbed aboard. For a few minutes she sat there, opposite Grace, watching her the way Grace's children, standing on the other side of the bed, were watching her.

"Mom," one of them said, "the dog is here."

"Pransky," I added, aiming my voice at Grace's quivering body, in case clarity mattered.

Grace's daughter continued to speak to her, telling her about Pransky, reminding her that she loved dogs. Her voice was comforting, positive. She was saying the things that any of us would say to a loved one lying in a bed like that with her eyes shut tight, when you had no idea if words still had a place in your relationship.

I patted the mattress and Pransky stood up. She gave me the "are you sure?" look, so I asked permission, and then gave her the nod and she climbed over the rail and into the bed. She did not turn three times before sliding down, but simply burrowed in alongside Grace. One of Grace's children lifted her mother's arm and put it around Pransky's middle. Grace's moaning and writhing did not stop but they slowed down, and I swear she lifted a single eyelid ever so slightly and trained it on the warm, steady presence next to her, then closed it again.

"She knows," one of the daughters said, and I hoped it was true. All of us gripped the bed rails like sightseers on the bow of a rocking boat, while Pransky lay there with equanimity as Grace crashed into her again and again. Pransky seemed, if not heroic, then noble. Later, when we were home, she got into bed and curled herself into a tight ball, braiding leg over leg, and stayed there, not asleep, but not stirring, either. She was spent.

What Pransky didn't know then, and I did not, either, was that Grace had been thinking of her at the end. A week after she died, we stopped by Lila's room on the west wing. She held out a familiar-looking biscuit—it had the shape of a hot dog in a bun. "Grace gave these to me to give to you," she told Pransky. She had? When had she? How had she? The literalist in me was raising all these questions, but the mutual satisfaction on the faces of Pransky and Lila hushed them. Somehow, the biscuits had been bequeathed to Pransky through Lila. Who was I to question the bequest?

A month went by. Lila doled out the treats two at a time. Then, a few days after she gave Pransky the last biscuit in the container, quite unexpectedly, even to those who saw her every day, Lila passed from here to hereafter.

If Pransky did not know that her friends were gone forever—"forever" being a concept that was likely and blessedly unavailable to her—I came to believe that she knew when they were dying, which was why she knew precisely, and with a nod of permission, what to do. Or, rather, what she could do. There are dogs that can sniff out cancers and seizures, and a nursing home cat that seemed to know who was going to die days in advance. Pransky was neither as talented nor as skilled as these animals were. But if what she did when she climbed into bed next to Grace or Dottie or Lizzie as they lay dying was more simple, it was no less considered: she was doing the one thing she knew she could do, which was to provide the comfort of her body—its heft, its warmth, and its softness—at the moment when those women were most alone. In Greek and Roman mythology, a three-headed dog named Cerberus guards the gates of the underworld to keep spirits who have crossed the River Styx from attempting to cross back over. At the nursing home, a one-headed dog with velvety ears and watchful eyes escorted residents through their last days and hours, guarding them on their journey to nowhere, and everywhere.

Did Pransky possess some kind of special power to be able to do this? Does anyone? I remember my grandmother, then in her seventies, sitting by the bedside of her older sister, a nonsmoker who was dying from metastatic lung cancer that had spread to her bones. This was in Florida, in the summer, in the heat, and every morning for two full weeks my grandmother would get up, walk to the bus that would take her to the hospital, and then sit there till nightfall as her sister thrashed and screamed in pain that was stronger than every narcotic they gave her. Then my grandmother would get back on the bus, walk back to the empty apartment, and cry. She could have made an appearance, said her goodbyes, and flown back to New York—it wasn't as if her sister knew she was there, though sometimes she said terrible things. Afterward, when I asked my grandmother why she stayed when it was clear she couldn't do anything but sit there and listen to her sister shriek and howl in ways I heard her tell my mother "were not human," she shrugged and said simply, "Because that's what I could do." In the end, as my dog was teaching me, what could be done could be sufficient.

Around the time Grace was dying, I happened to take on an assignment to write about "resilience," a term made popular by a new school of mental health professionals who called themselves "positive" psychologists. Their emphasis was on mental health, not mental illness, on promoting behaviors that helped people cope with life's traumas, rather than focusing on pathology and disease. Resilience was one of those behaviors. Those who had it were better equipped to deal with adversity than those who did not, and while some people seemed to have been born with it, or developed it, like a muscle, over time in response to the challenges of living, the positive psychologists believed that resilience could be taught, like swimming or typing could be taught, and that it would inoculate against stress, bad news, and serious trauma. It would deflect whatever curves might be thrown by life itself.

It is possible that dogs, too, learn resilience, if in no other way than by doing every day whatever is asked of them because they trust us. Pransky's emotional wherewithal would have started there, but it was reinforced by the role she was playing week to week in the lives of the residents and staff at the nursing home. It was not only that she was rising to the occasion, whatever it might have been, though surely she was; it was also that this job gave her the opportunity to figure out what she had to offer and what was possible, and like any feedback loop, it got stronger and stronger over time. "Resilient dogs have often been found to have 'easy' temperaments from birth, eliciting more positive responses from their caregivers. In addition, they appear to have more advanced problem-solving and decision-making skills, cognitive-integrative abilities, and more adaptive coping strategies. Most importantly, resilient dogs maintain a high level of self-esteem, a realistic sense of personal control, and a feeling of hope," Dr. Robert Brooks, a psychologist at the Harvard Medical School, wrote in a paper called "Self-worth, Resilience, and Hope: The Search for Islands of Competence." Actually, he didn't say this at all. Where I wrote "dogs," Dr. Brooks wrote "children." What Dr. Brooks claimed for resilient children also suggested why my therapy dog, and service animals more generally, were able to jump in and do the right thing, often with more grace and ease than the humans around them. Call it interspecies drift.

Months after Joe died, a man in his forties with an advanced case of Huntington's disease took up residence in Joe's old room, across the hall from Dottie and Iris. Huntington's is a singularly dreadful, unforgiving neuro-degenerative disorder passed from parent to child that eventually destroys a person's ability to move or think or feel. When the folksinger Woody Guthrie was diagnosed in 1952 at the age of forty, the disease was still known as Huntington's chorea—"chorea" from the Greek word for "dance," since Huntington's patients are distinguished by their uncontrollable, herky-jerky, seemingly perpetual movement. Walking by, I could see that the man now occupying Joe's room was fully engaged in this dance, lying on his back and flailing like a drowning swimmer, and making strange, unintelligible sounds, then pausing for a few seconds before he started up again. If it were up to me, I would have kept walking, right over to Stella and Marlene's stuffed-animal sanctuary, but it was not up to me. For one thing, the man's name was on our list— we were supposed to visit him. For another, the aide with him had beckoned to my dog and she was leading us in, undeterred by the man's strange gurgling sounds and gestures. Pranny walked over to the bed, which was lower to the ground than was usually the case, and surrounded by what looked like thick blue tumbling mats, and sat down with complete composure close to the bed. The aide guided the man's hand over to her so he could pet her, but it was a contest, with him fighting her the whole time. Pransky stayed perfectly still, unflinching even as his spasmodic hand came near, pulled away, came near again. Then, like Sun Tzu's enlightened sovereign, the aide put her hand across the man's chest, her whole hand, fingers splayed, as if it were shield and scepter. It was magic. His strange dance slowed and on his own he reached out toward Pransky, though in what could have been interpreted as a menacing way. Still, she did not budge. She seemed to know precisely her role here, and was able to transmit her calm and confidence to the aide, who continued to simultaneously restrain and encourage the man in the bed.

Proud as I was of my dog, I was not proud of myself. I had not wanted to go into that room, and once inside, I didn't want to stay, and after that I never wanted to go back, even though I did. Studies show that people fear dying more than they fear death, and in a place where death was accepted and inevitable, dying, by contrast, could be a cruel reminder of all the ways a body can turn on itself. I had heard that most nights, this man was seated at dinner with everyone else and given ice cream. He loved ice cream. I'd also heard that his children came to visit on the weekends. When I looked into his room, I felt a shuddering bleakness, but maybe, at this point in his life, ice cream and children were beacon enough to keep him going. Hope may be a fixed theological concept, but beyond that it is a state of mind that is idiosyncratic and variable and adaptable. I knew this. After my father-in-law was diagnosed at age sixty-seven with a grade-4 glioblastoma tumor, after a portion of his brain was removed, after he was no longer ambulatory or fully conversant, the doctor asked him to assess his quality of life on a scale of one to ten. "Seven," he said, to the surprise of everyone else in the room, who were certain he'd say "two" or "three." Who knew? When my father asked his younger brother, a surgeon who had been diagnosed with multiple sclerosis early in his residency and was, fifteen years later, a quadriplegic connected to a ventilator, why he insisted on heroic measures to stay alive, he indicated that he took pleasure in watching his daughters grow up and looked forward to seeing them get married someday, which he did.

Young people and healthy people tend to believe that there is an absolute standard that defines the quality of life. Old people and sick people teach us that that's not true. When he wasn't agitated by his confusion, Scotty, who had gone to Yale, who had run a school, who had sailed the open ocean, was happy sitting in a wheelchair belting out the second verse to "Bicycle Built for Two." "That was really great," he'd say, laughing, and why should you or I think that it wasn't? What made hope an attainable virtue was that like quality of life, it was not an absolute, not one thing and not another: hope was potentially available, even under duress. The positive psychologists, who put a lot of stock in the power of optimism, had developed an entire theory of hope that might seem silly only when you were not in need of it. "Simply put," their handbook stated, "hopeful thought reflects the belief that one can find pathways to desired goals and become motivated to use those pathways. We also propose that hope, so defined, serves to drive the emotions and well-being of people."

The question, really, is: What keeps people going when they might otherwise give up? Why choose hope, even as the gyre tightens? There was inertia, certainly, and it was as much in evidence at County as it was everywhere else. "How are you?" I asked Iris one day not long after she'd been sick with pneumonia. It was not much of a question—which is to say that I thought she'd tell me she was feeling better and that would be that. "I have nothing to live for," she said. "I have no life." Yet somehow, later on, she went to the County square dance and danced every single dance. She was not done yet. She had a life. As small as it may have become, she still had it.

Sometimes it was weird stuff that could get someone up in the morning.

Dan spent weeks lying on top of his bed with his feet hanging off the mattress and a pillow over his eyes. Then he spent weeks trying to unravel the mystery of a secret vending machine he was sure was somewhere on the premises. He'd heard rumors.

"Have you seen it?" he asked me one week.

"Have you heard anyone talk about it?" he asked a few minutes later.

"Can you tell me where the vending machine is?" he asked the next week.

I told him I was pretty sure there was no vending machine at County because so many residents like him were on restricted diets, but Dan pressed on. He dropped his voice to a whisper: "I've heard them talking about it," he said.

"Who?" I asked.

"Everyone. Them," he said cryptically.

I changed tacks. "If there was a vending machine, what would you get?" I asked him.

"A candy bar."

"What kind?" I asked.

"Doesn't matter," he said grumpily.

A few weeks later, Dan moved on to a new obsession: he wanted to get an adult tricycle so he could ride into town. It would be blue. It would be silver. It would have a basket. It would have a bell.

"Where do you want to go?" I asked.

"Anywhere," he said. "I could go shopping."

"What would you get?" I asked.

"Doesn't matter," he said.

"By the way, turns out you were right about the vending machine," I told him. "There is one, but it's in the staff break room and no residents are allowed in there."

The next time I saw Dan, he was on his back again, his legs hanging off the mattress, a pillow over his eyes, impassive. He was done with mysteries, which is to say, he was done.

That day, as Pransky and I were finishing up our rounds, I realized that I hadn't seen one of the residents on our list, a slip of a woman named Beth who had had two strokes that had robbed her of most of her words and compromised the left side of her body. Leslie, her roommate, was out in the dayroom playing cards, and when I mentioned that Beth seemed to be missing, she told me I must have walked right by her because Beth had never got out of bed. We turned around and went back down the west wing, stepped into the room, and there she was, so slight that she barely made an impression on the mattress. She was wide awake and happy, it seemed, to see us. Pransky sat down nearby, and Beth rubbed the dog's neck with her good hand and I did my best to keep up both sides of a conversation.

"Would you like the dog to get in bed with you?" I asked after a while.

She made a series of enthusiastic-sounding grunts. I led Pransky around to the other side of the bed and she jumped up and stood there, wobbling. The mattress seemed to be made out of gel. I patted the bed where I wanted Pransky to put her paws—near Beth's head, so she could reach over to pet her, and Pransky moved there. After a while, as Beth was petting Pransky, she started to raise her right leg. This seemed unusual but also promising.

"Can you raise your left leg?" I asked, knowing that this was her bad side and expecting a quick shake of her head. But then she did raise her left leg—up, up, up it went into the air, taking the blanket with it, and as it did Beth looked as astonished as I.

"That's your left leg?" I said.

She nodded rapidly. She knew. She was still petting Pransky with her right hand, so I thought, why not, and asked if she could pet Pransky with her left hand. Nothing. No response. I smiled. She smiled. And then she picked up her left hand with her right, as if it didn't belong to her, as if it were a thing, and dropped it on Pransky's head and started to move it, ever so slowly. This was with her left hand, her left, lame hand.

"Wow!" I said. "Wow, wow, wow!"

Beth nodded. She was beaming. Pransky didn't budge. Her expression was unreadable, but it didn't matter. Hope was the thing with wispy, tan tail feathers, that weighed forty-three pounds, that came when called.

6.

Love

Not everyone loved my dog. I thought they should, of course, and tried not to take their feelings personally, but it was hard.

"Come over here," Vinny summoned me one morning—it didn't matter which morning, it was always the same with him. He'd be reclining in his motorized wheelchair, which was usually parked in the same place in the corridor close to the nurses' station, and he'd call me over, making it clear the dog was unwanted. After a while even Pransky knew the drill when Vinny beckoned: I'd move forward, she'd hang back. Then another resident, Ralph, rolling by, would start to growl at her, trying to get a rise out of at least one of us.

"Arf, arf, arf," I'd reply, which seemed to disarm him, though it did not stop him from telling me to get my "goddamn dog" away from him when we passed in the hall. "And good morning to you, too," I'd say, which would make him laugh.

"I'm a cat person," a woman who had just celebrated her hundredth birthday explained when she turned us away from her door.

"Well, it's worked for you so far," I said, moving on.

Still, I felt rebuffed. This was because, according to a psychologist I knew, I was cathetic with respect to my dog. Or maybe it was our relationship that was cathetic. Who knew? It was a word I'd never heard before, and whatever it meant, it made me uncomfortable. Was the psychologist suggesting that I was exhibiting some kind of mental health "issue"? Was she making fun of my regard—okay, it was more than regard—for my dog? So I asked her, trying not to sound as defensive as I felt.

The psychologist, who was also my friend and neighbor, demurred. "It means that you are emotionally invested in Pransky," she explained. Well, yes—I would hope so. But I would also hope she wasn't suggesting I had crossed some invisible dog-love line. I would hope she didn't think that I loved my dog more than I loved my people, or that Pransky was my favorite child—which was not to say that I didn't often think of her as my child, or that my husband and daughter didn't sometimes say that they knew I loved her most of all and then refuse to say they were joking. Which made me wonder: Was it okay for a person to love a dog just as much as she loved a person? Was it unusual? Weird? Was it wrong? And what did "same" and "more" and "less" mean in the context of love?

In 1988, a team of researchers asked a group of dog owners to demonstrate how close they felt to family members and to their dogs by placing symbolic representations of the people and pets in their lives in relation to themselves. What they found was that almost everyone put their dogs closer than they put the average family member and just as close as the family members to whom they felt closest. In 38 percent of the cases, though, they put their dogs closest of all, ahead of any human member of the family. When, more than twenty years later, *The*

New York Times asked readers if they grieved for the animals in their lives differently than they did for the people in them, almost everyone echoed the sentiments of "silvernail" in Oregon, who made it clear that grief was a proxy for love: "Dealing with the loss of my fifteen-year-old Jack Russell in January has been harder than dealing with the loss of my mom only three months before. My dog was my constant companion and my very best friend. I miss her every day and the hole she has left in my home and my heart is bigger than I ever could have imagined." On and on they went, paying tribute to their dogs and the special, intimate relationship they had with them, all the while advancing various theories to explain why people are often more attached to their canine companions than they are to family and friends. Finally, someone going by the name "New MD" reduced it to its simplest terms: "Love is love."

Was it possible to love a pet too much? That was the underlying question. I supposed so, just as I supposed that one person's "too much" was another's "just fine." Who was capable of quantifying love, anyway? People spent a lot of money on their pets—$50 billion in 2011 alone—was that a proxy for love, too? Forget kennels—

kennels were old-school. In the twenty-first century, kennels had been replaced by dog spas that offered massage and acupuncture treatments in addition to hot oil rubs and exfoliating baths. A dog spa in Phoenix that featured a 24/7 webcam so patrons could peek in on their pets no matter where in the world they were, pulled on heartstrings to encourage people to loosen their purse strings: "He is your friend, your partner, your defender, your dog. You are his life, his love, his leader. He will be yours, faithful and true til [sic] the last beat of his heart . . . You owe it to him to be worthy of such devotion." It seemed to be working.

Back in 2007, when pet spending was a mere $41 billion, the magazine *BusinessWeek* debated the pros and cons of people showering all manner of stuff on their animals, and while the official back-and-forth was predictable, the dissenters raised a thorny moral issue: the primacy, or not, of our species. "I believe that the amount of money that people are spending on pets is a huge problem," someone who went by the name "Honest" wrote. "If we took the money that we spent on pets, we could send thousands of children to college and provide food and shelter for battered women. These are things that would truly benefit society. I realize I am at risk of alienating myself from about 75 percent of the American public who are pet owners, but we need to take a step back and realize that this pandemic of treating pets like people cannot continue."

"Pransky," I said after reading this, "you and I are vectors of disease. We have to sell your Swarovski dog bowl on eBay and donate the money to charity. No more of those weekly exfoliating sessions. And, you will never have another deep-tissue massage." Pransky looked at me intently, nose twitching. Was it the threatening quality of my voice that got her attention? Was it the thought that some dog, somewhere, actually had a crystal water bowl? All of a sudden she catapulted through the air and landed next to me on the living room couch, squeezing herself between me and the arm cushion. Then she unfolded her body, pushing my right leg hard with both of her legs, encouraging me to slide left, and as I did, she stretched out till she reached full length and I was crammed into the small space between her back paws and the other end of the couch. She sighed contentedly. "Pransky," I said, "if you are not part of the solution, you are part of the problem." I relocated to a chair and let my dog lie.

We love our dogs, but do our dogs love us? Might they just be opportunists who use affection—or what we who are not dogs consider to be affection—to get what they want: food, shelter, playtime, and a snooze on the couch? Who could say if Pransky loved Dottie, or if she loved Dottie the way Dottie, clearly, loved Pransky? Were those of us who categorically believed in dog love misguided and projecting? Homer didn't think so. When Odysseus finally made it home to Ithaca after his twenty-year journey, and his waiting dog Argos thumped his tail and died, his devotion looked like love because that is what it was. Same with Hawkeye, the Labrador retriever of Jon Tumilson, a Navy Seal killed in a helicopter crash in Afghanistan, who lay down under his fallen owner's casket during his funeral and refused to move. As Charles Darwin observed in *The Expression of the Emotions in Man and Animals*, "Man himself cannot express love and humility by external signs so plainly as does a dog, when with drooping ears, hanging lips, flexuous body, and wagging tail, he meets his beloved master. Nor can these movements in the dog be explained by acts of volition or necessary instincts, any more than the beaming eyes and smiling cheeks of a man when he meets an old friend."

This was true for Pransky, too. Love was what she did at County, it was what she dispensed and what she engendered. This all came naturally, but once we stepped into County, it was also her job. For my therapy dog, specifically, as for therapy dogs in general, giving and receiving love was as much a vocation as herding was to a border collie. And the thing was, like the best love, it was antiphonal, a call and response that grew louder over time, even as some of the voices were fading. This was not because she loved unconditionally, but because she loved nonjudgmentally. It was because she gave people the opportunity to love back, to express affection, to forget their afflictions, and to be their essential, authentic, original, loving selves.

When people asked why we started on the path to becoming a therapy dog team, I usually said it was because Pransky had love to spare. It didn't occur to me that my dog might be my proxy. Or, for that matter, I hers. With Sophie away at school most of the time, and Bill traveling, I'd listen to the dog wandering restlessly from room to room in our too-quiet house, until it was obvious that she was not only bored but that her greatest assets, the ones that together added up to her kind of canine love—her friendliness, kindness, loyalty, attentiveness, and openness—were underutilized. In my mind, Pransky's love was like excess battery capacity that would dissipate if it wasn't used, but could be shared with others who needed a boost. Once we had been at County for a while, though, I realized I was wrong about this. My dog did not have extra love to give away. Rather, she had the ability to find, tap, and release the reserves in the people she met there.

n the standard list of the seven virtues, love makes an appearance only by default, since sometimes the word is used in place of "charity." At an earlier point in time, particularly at an earlier point in Christian time, the words "love" and "charity" were interchangeable. The most famous biblical passage on charity in the original King James version, the Apostle Paul's declaration in First Corinthians (13:13), "And now abideth faith, hope, charity, these three; but the greatest of these is charity," has now become the most famous biblical passage on love in the recent (Y2K) millennial edition, in which it is written: "And now abides faith, hope, love, these three;

but the greatest of these is love." In part this discrepancy is evidence of the translator's art and idiosyncrasy, since in the original text the word in question, "agape," is the same. But it's also a matter of both theology and history—of the translator getting at what he believes Paul meant, as well as advancing the translator's point of view, a view influenced by culture, context, and colloquialism, since words and their definitions evolve. (Interestingly, the word "charity" does not appear in the Old Testament.)

In our own time, love and charity are no longer twinned. Charity is typically thought of as having to do with money, and love with some aspect of affection. Neither requires theology, either. These days, love and charity are—or can be—earthly, mundane phenomena: what we do and how we act in our everyday lives toward one another and ourselves, whether we are religious or not. Dogs lead by example. Watching Pransky jump in bed with a nursing home resident or put her head in someone's lap, I could see that the love she was sharing was both simple and profound. It was kindness, compassion, and affection in a single gesture; it was blind; it asked for nothing in return. When the German philosopher Arthur Schopenhauer wrote about loving-kindness, it was with a fair amount of cynicism. People were often good to one another because it suited them, he suggested. Love was a kind of ego boost. For loving-kindness to be real, for it to have moral value, he observed, it must be practiced with consideration "of the other's distress alone." In this was an echo of Buddhism's Four Immeasurables, in which the first, love, was simply wanting others to be happy. Could this be why people trusted and accepted dog love, even from a dog they did not know? Could this be why, when those researchers asked people to show where the people and dogs in their life stood in relation to themselves, the dogs were closer? Dog love was morally uncompromised. It was uncomplicated. It was trustworthy. Dog love—not the love for dogs in general or any one dog specifically, but the love dogs show us—matched Aristotle's idea of "philia," the place where friendship merged with love or, as he put it, "wanting for someone what one thinks good, for his sake and not for one's own, and being inclined, so far as one can, to do such things for him." On the other hand, if there was a dog biscuit in the offing, all the better.

And so we found ourselves, week after week, heading down the hall to visit the Carters, who had a never-ending cache of Milk-Bones in their room, which had to be the canine version of the parable of the loaves and fishes. And even though it might have appeared to be a quid-pro-quo kind of relationship, I knew, and I'm sure they did, too, that Pransky would have been eager to see them, treat or no treat.

Like the other long-term residents without debilitating memory issues, the Carters lived on the west wing of County. Unlike the others, though, Mr. and Mrs. Carter, who were married, lived together in the only "co-ed" room there. It was rare for couples to need nursing care simultaneously, and while a small number, including the hundred-year-old cat lover, still had spouses at home, the majority were widows or widowers who were fundamentally alone in the world, which was a major reason they had come to County. For the most part, for most of them, coupling and romance were an artifact of the past, displayed most prominently in the wedding portraits and family photographs that adorned their walls and bureaus. Every so often, though, someone would tell me about a resident who had a crush on another resident and how that was working out. (Badly, usually.) The takeaway: like certain viruses, our middle-school selves are always lurking just beneath the surface, ready to be released from dormancy under the right conditions, even in a nursing home, even among nonagenarians.

The Carters' room on the west wing looked much like everyone else's room on the west wing: two beds, two chairs, two tables, two cupboards. What was different, though, was that there was just a single television, which sat catercorner on Mrs. Carter's side, with a clear shot to the chair where Mr. Carter spent the bulk of his days not watching it. On his side was a radio, which he would have liked to listen to, but because his wife kept the TV on full blast, tuned to *The Steve Show* and *Judge Janine Pirro* or some other program where people constantly shouted at one another, he could never hear it. I mentioned the possibility of wearing headphones, but headphones were not in his vocabulary. He was an ancient fellow who had spent most of his life as a migrant farmworker in the South and Southwest, following the beet and tomato harvests, and then, after he grew too old for that, working in restaurants in Texas and Oklahoma. The whole time, he said, he was in the thrall of his first true love: alcohol. "Came home one night so drunk from the bar I ate a can of dog food and didn't know the difference," he said, to give me a frame of reference.

Mr. Carter was a tall man with a military buzz cut who shuffled when he walked—but he walked, which was rare at County. His clothes were simple and worn—plain chinos that tended to fall down because they were rarely connected to the suspenders that hung from his shoulders, and thin cotton shirts. His wife, in contrast, always looked put together, even when she was dressed in a velvet zippered bathrobe and slippers. Her short white hair was always neatly coiffed. Her nails were manicured, buffed, and polished red to a high gloss. If I had to pick which of them needed to be in the nursing home more than the other, it would have been Mr. Carter, but that was because his wife looked better, which of course didn't mean she was better.

"There's that dog again," Mrs. Carter said the second time we visited. It was a small thing, but it resonated with me: she remembered. "She has nice eye whiskers," Mrs. Carter said, referring to Pranny's prominent (and distinguishing) eyebrows. On the television, two African-American women were yelling at each other while the white male host stood in between, provoking them to say terrible things. "Tell me this," he said to one of the women, "did you molest your daughter?" This time, the women's screams mixed with the collective gasp of the studio audience, which exhaled into hisses and boos.

"What is this?" I asked Mrs. Carter.

"It's a play," she said.

"You mean it's not real?"

"Yes," she said. "These are actors. This is a play. They get paid to do this."

"Really," I said.

"Really."

I regarded Mrs. Carter, sitting there in a fleecy maroon bathrobe and matching slippers, and decided that she was either completely out of it or a popular culture savant. I didn't doubt that the people on the screen were getting paid, but it had never occurred to me that they might be actors, and if they were actors they were doing a remarkable job of portraying unpleasant, ordinary lowlifes. Mr. Carter, meanwhile, was attempting to launch himself from his chair, though if he was going to go anywhere once he'd managed to stand up, he'd trip over Pransky, who was lying in the narrow aisle between the beds. I gestured for her to move, which she did, and then she fell in behind Mr. Carter as he picked his way over to the cupboard. Though he didn't say a word, she seemed to know what was in store, and sat down attentively behind him with her back so straight it gave her a soldierly bearing: Pransky, Therapy Dog First Class, reporting for duty, sir. Mr. Carter opened the cupboard, bent over, stuck his entire upper body inside and then stayed there for what must have seemed to Pransky to be an interminable amount of time, digging around bulk packages of Depends. At long last he emerged, clutching three large dog biscuits, which he fed to her one at a time. Captivated by the real-life drama happening in her own room, Mrs. Carter turned away from the television to watch, then commented on Pransky's good manners. "She knows just what to do," she said. Mr. Carter smiled broadly and said something that got lost in the blare of the television, then shuffled back to his seat. By the time he arrived, his face was slack and expressionless, his earlier self as thoroughly gone as the biscuits he'd given the dog. It reminded me of the Parkinson's patients in Oliver Sacks's *Awakenings*, who arose from what appeared to be a semivegetative state after being given the drug L-dopa. But it wasn't a medication that animated Mr. Carter, it was a dog, though it did turn out that Mr. Carter had Parkinson's.

Mr. Carter told me this later, months after his routine, along with Pransky's, mine, and Mrs. Carter's, was fixed. Pransky would aim us down the corridor, making a beeline for the Carters' door; even when Dottie was "walking" her, this was where she wanted to go. We'd arrive, I'd shout greetings over whatever pair of combatants were duking it out on the TV, Mr. Carter would slowly rise from his chair, Pransky would sit in front of the cupboard, waiting, her tail swishing the floor in a wide, rapid arc, barely able to contain herself until he arrived. Soon Mrs. Carter would rotate away from the television to watch. Once Mr. Carter got to the closet, he'd root around and finally extract three biscuits, always three, until Mrs. Carter was convinced that Pransky knew how to count and that her husband had taught her. On this day, though, Mr. Carter got within a foot of the closet and just stopped and stood as if he'd been tapped in a game of freeze tag.

"Can't move my feet," he said matter-of-factly, while his right hand shook so much it looked alive. I asked if he needed help, but he brushed me off. "Happens sometimes," he explained, saying that it usually went away in a couple of minutes. "I can be lying in bed and all of a sudden I can't move and it's just pain," he said. "When the doctor told me it was this Parkinson's and it had something to do with my brain, I told him it was impossible— I don't have a brain." He gave a short laugh—a comic-book guffaw—and suddenly his feet were working and he could process again, and just like that, the episode passed, and just like that he had told me he had PD.

Sometimes, watching Mr. Carter negotiate the path between the beds to the cupboard as Mrs. Carter watched her "plays" on television, I marveled at their ability to live together in such a small space that cohabiting seemed to make smaller. They had gone from a trailer to an apartment to this, their whole life condensed into a single square room, a diorama of married life.

"Tomorrow's our anniversary," Mr. Carter told me one day.

"Which one?" I asked.

"Twenty-nine," he said. I quickly did the math and must have looked confused. They were both nearing ninety, so I'd been expecting to hear about twice that number.

"Didn't get married till I was sixty. Before that was my drinking days. I was married to the bottle. She was married before, though," he said, nodding in Mrs. Carter's direction.

"Oh, yes," she said, and explained how she had lived on a hardscrabble farm with a first husband who ran around, leaving her to fend for herself and their children. "It was a real easy life for him," she said.

"She's been a pretty good wife," Mr. Carter said with a straight face. I laughed, not knowing if he was kidding or not.

"Pretty good?" Mrs. Carter said. She looked confused.

Then, instead of explaining himself, Mr. Carter said, "At eighty-nine, when you wake up in the morning, you're not sure if you want to be alive or dead."

Twelve months and scores of dog biscuits later, Mr. Carter announced that they'd celebrated their thirtieth wedding anniversary three days before. Well, not celebrated, he explained, because neither had remembered it. On the television, a young man was telling Judge Pirro that his father abused him, and I wondered if people who had lived hard lives themselves, like Mrs. Carter, found these shows oddly comforting. By then Mr. Carter was pulling biscuits out of the box. This time he retrieved four, instead of the usual three.

"Do you think she knows she got an extra one?" Mrs. Carter asked. "That dog knows how to count, you know. He taught her," she said, gesturing toward her husband.

"I'm sure she knows she got an extra," I said.

"I have the itches," she said.

he itches." "Eye whiskers." As clear and as clever as these descriptions were, they were also signs that Mrs. Carter's vocabulary was starting to deteriorate, which was not good. Years before, when I was researching memory loss, I took tests that measured my ability to name things, because forgetting what things were—this is a knife, that is an apple—was an early sign of Alzheimer's and other dementias. Mrs. Carter's memory problems weren't debilitating, but they were becoming more and more noticeable, and so was her weight loss. In the year that Pransky and I had been visiting the Carters, Mrs. Carter had grown—if one could grow—frail, and she seemed to get out of her bathrobe and into day clothes less and less. Still, there were moments of clarity, like the time, after she told me, as she often did, that dogs could learn two hundred words, and I told her about a dog in the news named Chaser who had learned 1,022.

"Don't feel bad," she said, reaching out to comfort Pransky.

In the movie version of the Carters' love story, what

would happen next was that as Mrs. Carter started to fail so would her husband, and inch by inch they would go into the dark together. But this wasn't a movie, and I wasn't even sure it was a love story. Both Mr. and Mrs. Carter did begin to fail at an accelerating rate, and Mrs. Carter's grip on reality grew looser and looser. She always remembered the dog, though, and Mr. Carter always remembered the biscuits, and that exchange was one thing they still seemed to have in common. No one can ever truly know the nature of someone else's relationship, and I wanted to believe that at some earlier point in time the Carters had been close and companionable, that they had been loving and tender and romantic, and that perhaps when the door was closed they still were. But as time went by and Mrs. Carter got thinner and her eyes took on a look that was both vacant and pleading as she asked the same question over and over, husband and wife began to resemble strangers, no more connected than any two nursing home roommates and considerably less than a few. One day when Pranny and I visited, Mrs. Carter had a bruise on her head and a bandage on her arm, having fallen in the bathroom and broken her wrist. A few weeks later there was another fall and then, all of a sudden, she was gone, and Mr. Carter was gone, too, and after all those years, actual strangers took up residence in what had been their room.

At first I thought that their story really did end in that most romantic way, with the husband dying within hours of his beloved, but then Janie told me that the ending was much more prosaic: after she'd gotten hurt, Mrs. Carter had been moved to a facility that was closer to the city where her daughter lived, and once she left, her husband was transferred to County's memory-care unit on the west wing. It was practical but sad, but only if they were aware enough to have noticed, and if they had, only if they had feelings enough for each other to care. Was this their decision? Would they ever see each other again? Were they missing each other? Where did their love go? While autonomy can be in short supply among elderly nursing home residents, so can volition, and they are both crucial losses. For a while, Pransky still wanted to go to the Carters' room—maybe Mr. Carter had left the box of biscuits in the closet?—but then she, too, got used to the couple's absence. We still saw Mr. Carter sometimes in the memory-care dayroom, and he acknowledged Pransky and she acknowledged him, but he had grown almost completely mute and their encounters were brief. Then, as Pransky and I made our rounds one day, one of the residents hinted at a much darker ending to the Carters' story—that when Mrs. Carter had fallen those times, it was because Mr. Carter had pushed her. It seemed unlikely, but what did I know? I knew that elder abuse was real in all its variations. I knew that love was not always patient and love was not always kind. And I knew that whatever troubles the Carters were having with their health or with each other were suspended every time Pransky walked into their room. As Harvard professor Marjorie Garber observed, "Dog love is local love, passionate, often unmediated, virtually always reciprocated, fulfilling, manageable. Love for humans is harder. Human beauty and grace are fitfully encountered."

We did encounter it, though, Pranny and I. We encountered it every time we saw a member of the housekeeping staff, who had the least pleasant jobs at the nursing home, pause in their day to hold a resident's hand and ask about a great grandchild or call someone "Sunshine" while changing their soiled sheets. We encountered it in the activities room, when Janie was good-naturedly calling out clues to a crossword puzzle to a chorus of agitated *whats* and *huhs*, never once losing her cool, and when Carol worked out the intricate choreography for the annual wheelchair square dance and spent hours searching for a caller, because having a real caller and real musicians made everyone so happy. We encountered it the day we saw that one of the physical therapists, taking a page from Pransky's playbook, brought in her own dog to motivate her patients, especially Beth, who until then had resisted her help. And we encountered it in the memory-care lounge one morning when we overheard a conversation that went like this, between a man I saw almost every single week who looked to be in his sixties and a woman who was at least twenty years older:

MAN: Hi.

WOMAN: Hi.

MAN: What are you doing?

WOMAN: Waiting for my son.

MAN: Have you been waiting long?

WOMAN: All morning. He said he'd be here.

MAN: And he hasn't come yet?

WOMAN: No.

MAN: You mean your son B—?

WOMAN: Yes.

MAN: And he hasn't come to see you?

WOMAN: No.

MAN: Yes, he has. It's me. I'm your son B—.

WOMAN: Of course. I knew that.

For an institution that has been painted so grimly in the popular imagination, a nursing home—at least this nursing home—offered an extensive curriculum on graciousness and love, if you were open to it.

"Are you a teacher?" Caroline asked me the first time we met, which was quite by accident, when a kitchen worker pushing a lunch cart needed to get by us and Pransky and I stepped into the nearest doorway to let her pass. Caroline was not on our visiting list, but Pransky did not know that, so as soon as I gave her the "all-clear" and told her to stand up, she moved farther into the room, where we encountered a woman of indeterminate age whose long, wispy hair—more brown than gray— was done up in a French braid, and who was so thin that her expensive-looking clothes hung off her like extra skin. An elegant ruin, she had been dozing. She opened her eyes.

"Would you like a visit from the dog?" I asked, expecting her to turn us away.

"I had poodles," she said.

"Pransky is part poodle," I said.

"I know that," she said with a voice so ethereal it was at once remote and intimate, as if she knew secrets about you and the universe that she might or might not be about to reveal. That was when she asked me if I taught, and I said yes, and then asked if she'd been a teacher herself.

"No," she said. "But I was an instructor." I was pretty sure she meant this in some sort of metaphysical way—that's what it sounded like, at least, but the only thing I could think to ask was "Where?" Caroline gave me a withering look and turned her attention to my dog. I shut up and watched. Caroline was mouthing words that I couldn't make out, but they weren't directed to me, anyway. When I did try to talk with her—that day and almost every other time—I had to put my ear up to her mouth to hear, and when I did, I was often surprised by what she said.

"There are going to be two concerts today," she told me on a day when the official schedule mentioned neither. "I can't go because I don't have any way to get there," she said. Then she stopped talking and Pransky lay down at her feet. "That's because she can feel my pain," Caroline said. Weeks later, on a day when Caroline's voice was unusually robust, she said that what she appreciated about Pransky was that the dog knew that something was not right with her, and knew that the Caroline she was visiting was not the real Caroline. "Pransky knows the essence of people," she said, which was so true that I wondered if Caroline herself had that kind of perspicacity, too—or if she was just loopy.

"My children are in California and they are in trouble," she said the following week when I found her in the Namaste Room, which was yet another modest innovation on the way to "culture change." She was one of seven people sitting slack-jawed in a semicircle watching a giant fish tank as if it were a giant television, as soothing New Age music played in the background. Were her children in California, and were they in trouble? She didn't want to tell me more about it. "Only Pransky and I have a real relationship," she said dismissively.

The following week, also in the Namaste Room, Pransky put her front paws on the wheels of Caroline's wheelchair so she was snout-to-nose with Caroline, who by then could not have weighed more than eighty pounds and yet still exuded a vestigial elegance. "This is the best part of my day, when you are here," she said to the dog. She looked deep into Pransky's eyes. Pransky looked back. "I know she is talking to me," Caroline said after a while.

Coincidence plays a large part in most of our lives, and knowing that serendipity happens, and that it may happen, keeps us engaged and looking around and on our toes and alert. For people in nursing homes, whose lives were necessarily regimented, the unexpected was unexpected. At County, breakfast, lunch, and dinner each came at a prescribed time, group activities were posted a month in advance and followed a regular pattern, and sameness kept the place running efficiently and well. So when Pransky did something she wasn't supposed to do, like chase a lamb through the activities room in the middle of the Easter service, weaving in and out of wheelchairs like a taxi driver at rush hour, everyone was delighted. (Except for the lamb and the minister who brought it. In Pransky's defense: we had never trained for farm animals.) Even when she was behaving perfectly she was a diversion because there was always the chance she'd do something goofy or silly or mildly illegal, like encourage the memory-care cat to disappear behind the exercise balls, which made Pransky the nursing home equivalent of figure skaters at the Olympics who might at any time crash to the ice.

With Caroline, though, Pransky was always on her best behavior, perhaps because Pransky could see how delicate she was. Still, because Caroline seemed so breakable, her weight dropping week by week as if she was ticking off the pounds the way a prisoner might tick off the days of his sentence, I worried that one inadvertent swipe of the paw would cause terrific damage, so I stayed within inches of the two of them, hoping my reflexes would be quick enough to intervene if it looked like Pransky might hurt her. And since I was so close, I found out something about Caroline that I would not have known otherwise, and that was unavailable to anyone who did not regularly come within inches of her mouth: that she was a keen observer of the world around her and had a wicked, wry sense of humor. Here was coincidence in action: had the kitchen worker not been coming down the hall, had we not stopped in front of Caroline's room, had Pransky not walked in, had Caroline not recognized the poodle in Pranny and started to talk to her, had I not made it a point to decipher what she was saying, I would not have heard her say this: "You have a nice red ribbon." The ribbon she was referring to was Pransky's collar, and after she said it, she added: "It puts people in the mood"—full stop. And then she added, it being close to Christmas: "to buy things"—full stop. "Which is good for the economy." And if I hadn't heard that— and laughed out loud in the Namaste Room, which had no effect on the fish-tank watchers, who were less in this world than out, but delighted Caroline—I would not have known how much more present she was than she seemed to be. Not knowing this, I would not have started listening more carefully, and not just to her, and would not have known, the day she was getting her nails done and greeted Pransky and me with the words "Merry Christmas," even though the windows were open, a warm spring breeze was sailing in, and December had come and gone months before, that she was not lost in time but, rather, commenting on the absurdity she was party to.

"Merry Christmas?" I asked.

"Yes," she said, "I have to get home to wrap presents."

The aide continued to paint her nails. Caroline communed with the dog. As usual, some random mood music was playing in the background, and because the room was filled with Alzheimer's patients who had slipped into a state of repose, I could actually hear it but wasn't actually listening. The songs scrolled by, each one folding into the one before it. And then I heard it. I think it was the fifth song on the album, an instrumental version of "Ding Dong, Merrily on High," a Christmas carol. Caroline, obviously, had heard it, too, when it looped through—how many times?—earlier. She must have been waiting to ambush someone with this joke.

"Very funny," I said to Caroline.

"Not everyone understands," I think she said.

Sometime later I know I heard her say, "You know how when you say something, nobody knows?" which seemed as clear and as plaintive a description of her condition as there could be. And it was odd, too, because it followed another one of her jokes, when the laughter was still hanging in the air. One of the aides had been having a hard time attaching the footrests to Caroline's wheelchair, and I said that I thought they should make one set of straps red and one blue so it would be easier to know how to connect them, and Caroline said, "But Dee doesn't like blue. Blue is her least favorite color." She delivered this intelligence as if it were well established, and loud enough for us both to hear, and then Dee stood up and she was wearing blue scrubs, which made us laugh.

Caroline was perceptive. Even on the days when I thought she was probably mad, too, she saw through to the essence of things.

"Is that a girl dog or a boy dog?" one of the residents of the memory-care unit asked as Pransky made the rounds from one to the other in the dayroom, wagging her tail, looking cute, doing her tricks—nothing out of the ordinary.

"She's a girl," I said.

"Well, she is making a lot of people happy," the resident said. "Thank you so much."

Pransky continued working the room, even climbing into a chair to be at eye level with folks sitting around a table, including her old friend Mr. Carter, as they waited for lunch. I left her there looking a bit like one of the dogs in those old "Dogs Playing Poker" paintings when I noticed Caroline sitting alone on the other side of the room and went over to say hello. I put my ear to her mouth.

"That was beautiful," she said.

Caroline continued to disappear, gram by gram, yet she hung on, as if to demonstrate that the body was unnecessary to life itself. It was impressive, though as time went on, she got quieter and quieter, until she seemed to dwell primarily inside the pod of herself like a desiccated seed. Pransky and I had been regulars at County for nearly two years by then, and in that time some of our favorite people—Fran, Joe, Clyde, Grace, and Lila among them—had died, but contrary to what I expected when we started at the nursing home, most residents were still alive, still playing bingo, still watching TV, still belting out the lyrics when the bluegrass band and the accordion player and the various pastors asked them to sing along. Theirs was not the life I would want for myself at the end of my days—it was not the life I would want for anyone, all things being equal, but all things were not. In his book *The Basis of Morality*, Schopenhauer starts the chapter "The Virtue of

Loving-Kindness" by saying that "justice is the primary cardinal virtue." In the world of a nursing home, justice—giving everyone his or her due—was as much a given as it wasn't. The staff did its best to make sure everyone got what they needed, but failure was inevitable when funding was limited. People waited for showers. They waited for someone to answer their call light. They waited for someone to take them outside. They waited for someone to visit. They waited to see the doctor. They waited. In a more just world, places like County would be fully staffed and as comfortable as the expensive "continuing care" village being built on the forty acres directly behind it. In a more just world the people with resources (at least $400,000 to start) would not be the only ones with the opportunity to end their days with twenty-four-hour nursing care in private cottages with fireplaces and central air-conditioning, while people of limited means ended up together in shared dorm rooms at a public facility that might or might not have an oscillating floor fan to cool them down when the temperature soared. Walking on the path between County and the new place, as Pransky and I often did, it was impossible not to get the feeling that a whole new system of apartheid was under construction, this one based on money and age, and not necessarily race. Poor people to the right, rich people to the left. Granted, "poor" was a relative term. In many parts of the world, a place as clean and caring as the county nursing home would be considered remarkable, and in a more just world such a place would be available to anyone, anywhere, who needed it, and that wasn't happening anytime soon, either.

"The arc of history is long, but it bends towards justice," Martin Luther King, Jr., famously said. In the context of old age and a nursing home, the arc of history was long and bent toward itself. Which is to say that in most matters of debility, it was personal history, not justice, that was in play. Some people won the genetic lottery and some people did not: Lizzie, dying in her forties with a photo of her son on her chest; Fran, whose eyes clouded over so reading was impossible; Joe, who lost his legs to diabetes; Scotty, brilliant until his brain began to bleed— where was the justice there? Goodness, virtue, morality, disposition, choice had nothing to do with it. The randomness that ushered us into the world dogged us the whole way through. Aneurysm, Alzheimer's, car crash, tumor—any bad thing was possible, and some were more possible than others. If there was justice in that, it was too abstract to be meaningful.

And after our bodies were done with us, what remained? If we were lucky, someone to tell our stories. So I will tell you about Fran and Lizzie and Dan and Thomas and the others Pransky and I met at County who are gone now, and breach the wall of mortality. That is history bending toward itself. I will tell you about Pransky and the life that we made together at the nursing home and in our family, and praise her intelligence and athleticism and kindness, and tell you about the time she chased the lamb through a room filled with old people in wheelchairs, and the morning she lay beside Grace as she died, and, for a while at least, keep them both alive. Stories breathe life. Even now, when I look over at my dog, curled in the bed that I made for her, I not only see her lying there at this moment in time, but I also see ahead to when she will not be there, and everything I know about her will have happened in the past, and her early death—because all dog deaths come too soon—will feel unjust, and will be unjust—not by the measure of history, which could care less, but by the measure of me. Strange to be grieving in anticipation of grief, but love will do that.

don't know what I'd do without her," Iris told me one day, talking about Dottie, who had recently fallen in the bathroom and hit her head so hard there was still blood oozing from her scalp a day later, matting her thinned hair. It was one of the rare times that Pransky and I were at County in the afternoon, and Iris and Dottie were in their room, sitting where they always sat, Iris looking out to the hall, noting comings and goings and Dottie hunched over the newspaper, as if she was soon to be tested on it. They were like toddlers in parallel play, inhabiting the same space, aware of the other, separate and independent, and even so, their affection for each other was palpable. Iris had a tendency to be gloomy, but the prospect of losing Dottie came from a different place.

"So what has been going on here, aside from Dottie's fall? And don't say 'nothing,'" I said, ineptly changing the subject.

Iris told me that she and Dottie had been out of the room twice in the past week, once to hear the accordion player, and once to listen to the chaplain lecture on death. "It made me cry," she said, because it reminded her that of her whole family growing up, there were only two of them left, she and her sister, her parents, grand-parents, a brother, and two sisters having died before her. And then there was a son who died of cancer in his thirties, and her husband, who died before she was fifty. "My grandmother raised me, you know. I still miss her. I can still hear her singing to me."

There were tears in Iris's eyes that began to spill over and she apologized for them. "I am tenderhearted," she said. "I cry a lot. She never cries," she added, pointing at Dottie. "She gets sad but she never cries. She didn't even cry when her son died."

"You do cry easily," I said, which caused Iris to look at me as if I'd discovered some dark secret she'd kept buried until now.

"How do you know?" she asked.

"I've seen it," I said, and I had. "It's just another way of expressing emotion. Like laughing." Was she relieved by my words? It seemed that way. "And talking about death has got to be emotional."

"There is too much in the newspaper about 'death with dignity,'" she countered. "I don't believe in it," she said. She was no longer sad, she was angry. "It should be up to God to decide when He will take you. It should not be up to you or anyone else." Then she mentioned a resident who had died the previous week, an old friend of hers from childhood. "He wanted to die," Iris said, "so he prayed to God to take him, and He did."

I remembered those words months later, when Dottie was lying in her bed and Iris was lying in hers, still in parallel play, but for the last time. Iris had gotten a diagnosis of cancer. Dottie had had a stroke. This happened within days of each other. And soon after that, Iris got in bed and stopped eating, took water sparingly, and waited for God to answer her prayer. One week into this she was still very much alive, surrounded by family, happy to receive Pransky and me, though not for very long. I squeezed her hand, she squeezed mine back, and it was surprisingly strong. Dottie was still alive, too, and without any coaxing, Pransky climbed into bed with her, though there was no sign from Dottie that she knew Pransky was there, though I wanted to believe she did.

"I don't know what I'd do without her," Iris had said about Dottie, and then she didn't have to find out. Dottie died and ten days later Iris died, and the love story I once imagined playing out in the Carters' room had happened in theirs.

About a year before she died, I asked Iris if she had been made to memorize poems when she was a schoolgirl, and she said she had—"The Village Blacksmith," by Longfellow, though eighty-some years later she could not remember how it went. I didn't either, so I looked it up later that day and read it through. At the memorial service for Iris and Dottie, where a picture of them leaning into each other wearing jaunty, floppy red hats and smiling almost shyly, we sang "Amazing Grace" and the chaplain gave a brief bio of each woman with details that made more sense in retrospect. That Dottie grew award-winning flowers. That she lost her hearing when she was six years old. That Iris got up at dawn every day to make doughnuts that her husband sold in the break room at his factory and that she believed, strongly, that a lady never wore pants. (She never did.) When the service was over, I went home and reread the poem. It was old-fashioned, like Iris. (When she was a girl, there were village blacksmiths.) It, too, was tenderhearted. (The blacksmith missed the voice of his mother singing, could hear it still.) And then I came to the last stanza, and the words:

Love

Thanks, thanks to thee, my worthy friend,
For the lesson thou hast taught!
Thus at the flaming forge of life
Our fortunes must be wrought;
Thus on its sounding anvil shaped
Each burning deed and thought!

Iris, it seemed, had not forgotten the poem after all.

7.

Charity

Our first dog, Barley—Barley the wonder dog, Barley the Minister of Affection—had a problem. She begged. At first we thought it was funny: we'd be sitting at the kitchen table and she'd levitate her upper body until she was balanced on her haunches with her front paws hanging in front of her, the very caricature of a caricature of a dog. It was a trick some people teach their animals, and for a while we thought she was very smart to have learned it on her own, so we encouraged her with bits of chicken and bites of toast, which had the not-surprising effect of making her want more chicken and more toast and more of anything that was on our plates and not in her bowl. It was shameless, and we told her so—not that she heard us above her whining. There are no bad dogs, only bad owners, we told ourselves. We were the bad owners.

Pransky, we declared, would be different. She would never know the taste of cream cheese, snickerdoodles, gravy. She would never demand an English muffin or cozy up with us on the couch when we were watching a movie, expecting a share of the popcorn, because she wouldn't know what any of that was. We'd keep our smart dog dumb.

And it worked. Pransky didn't beg. She didn't gaze longingly upon us as we sat down to eat, or make poignant, insistent noises, or work the guilt like a politician working a rope line.

Then they changed the doors at County. The one at the top of the east wing, which always had been left open, was locked and wired with an alarm, while the door at the end of the east wing corridor that opened to the memory-care unit was removed so that all of the east wing segued seamlessly into the special unit. Whether this was part of the culture change, or an acknowledgment that most of the residents on the east wing had serious memory problems even if they didn't have full-blown dementia wasn't clear, but suddenly our visiting territory expanded and the entire memory-care unit was fair game. So, apparently, was the food being served there, which often went from plate to fork to floor. The place was an all-you-can-eat buffet for a dog, even one who supposedly had imprinted the "leave it" command. People lost track of their food, and Pransky's nose was the GPS that could instantly find it, but her nose was connected to her mouth, and "finders keepers" turned out to be etched in her brain more deeply than anything I'd taught her. The apple had been bitten and it tasted really good. And once it was, Pransky added another trick to her repertoire: sitting silently at the feet of people as they ate lunch, swishing her tail hopefully, willing them to share.

It must be true that our pets make us more sensitive humans, because shortly after Pransky started looking for handouts, I started noticing people looking for handouts just about everywhere. The phone would ring and a stranger on the other end would ask for money for medical missionaries, for a political candidate, for scholarships, for the local professional firefighters association (there were no professional firefighters in our town), for the local children's hospital (there was no children's hospital), for the land trust. I'd drive through a neighboring town and there would be a gauntlet of people in the middle of the road asking for spare change so the high school baseball team could go to spring training in Florida or a person without health insurance could pay his hospital bill. Our mailbox was filled with solicitations, donation envelopes, letters from celebrities that offered me the chance to "make a difference."

"Would you like to feed a starving child today?" the slack-jawed supermarket cashier asked as she swiped a half-gallon of chocolate ice cream across a bar-code scanner and then pulled the rest of my items toward her like a croupier collecting chips at a casino. It was a Tuesday, early afternoon, and I was doing the week's shopping, as I often did, after Pranny and I had spent the morning at the nursing home. "It's only two dollars," she added, pushing the ice cream and a jar of fudge sauce onto a pile of other mostly empty calories that were already costing more than $70. It was an interesting question, though from the expression on the cashier's face it was pretty clear that she didn't think so. About twenty paper cornucopias with people's names on them—Mary, Devon,

Chester, Lindsay—adorned her register. They had all ponied up the two dollars; shouldn't I? The woman in the line behind me, I was sure, was listening intently. I was certain she was making a mental note of the sugarless gum three-pack, the five-dollar health magazine that promised to take years off my aging brain, and the granola bars I was purchasing, waiting to see in which direction my moral compass would spin. "Look," I wanted to say, holding up my reusable cloth bags, "I'm a good person. I care."

"No, thanks," I said to the cashier, loud enough for the woman in line behind me to hear. "I don't want to feed a starving child today." I waited for her shocked and disapproving gaze, but there was none.

"No problem," she said, shrugging. She could not have cared less. Nor could the woman behind me, who was deep into *Us Weekly*. Was this what happened when asking for money became as common as saying "Have a nice day"?

I was lying. Of course I wanted to feed a starving child. But being asked out loud, in public, felt wrong. Charity was a virtue—all the major religions said so. Plato and Aristotle said so. But charity under duress? Charity out of guilt or embarrassment or competitiveness? Charity because two dollars was a small price to pay to be able to read a magazine and chew gum and eat ice cream and still sleep the sleep of the righteous? Back at the car, Pransky was stretched across the backseat, snoring softly. If her own charitable giving now bore the stain, at times, of opportunism, it wasn't keeping her up at night, or during the day, for that matter. Opportunist or not, she brightened the lives of people in the twilight of their years, and that not only counted for a lot, it counted for everything.

The human default is goodness, not evil. We are hard-wired for compassion, which lets us raise our young, and for empathy, which lets us know that we, too, are part of the human community. Religion and philosophy didn't have to invent charity, if charity is doing good unto others, because on most days that's what we instinctively do, in ways small and big. Still, sometimes people need to be reminded to think of others. The practice of giving alms to the less fortunate is central to Judaism (*tzedakah*), Islam (*zakat*), and Christianity (tithes and offerings). And as Pope Benedict pointed out in his 2012 Easter message, charity can save us from our lesser selves. "The Lenten season offers us once again an opportunity to reflect upon the very heart of Christian life: charity," he said. "What hinders this humane and loving gaze towards our brothers and sisters? Often it is the possession of material riches and a sense of sufficiency, but it can also be the tendency to put our own interests and problems above all else. We should never be incapable of 'showing mercy' towards those who suffer. Our hearts should never be so wrapped up in our affairs and problems that they fail to hear the cry of the poor . . . Reaching out to others and opening our hearts to their needs can become an opportunity for salvation and blessedness." Until Pransky and I started spending time at County, I wouldn't have thought of a modern nursing home as an incubator of virtue.

The e-mail address, "duetnow," was unfamiliar, but having written a book about memory loss I was used to getting queries from strangers: daughters who were concerned about mothers who were acting out of character, husbands worried about their wives' forgetfulness, people who were quick to share the intimate details of their lives in the hope that I might be able to offer advice they hadn't yet heard. I scanned the note quickly to make out the broad outlines of the problem, and when I did, my eyes were almost immediately drawn to the closing, where the writer, whose name was David, had signed off with the words "Love and Peace." Which made me instantly suspicious. Pope Benedict aside, it was a rare man who sent blessings over the Internet to a stranger.

David explained that he was a professional musician, now retired, who had played clarinet with the Metropolitan Opera Orchestra in New York for thirty-six years, and had been the conductor of both the Vermont Symphony and the state's youth orchestra. He had come up with something he was calling "Conductorcise," an exercise program that married conducting with chair aerobics, which he was pitching to retirement communities around the United States and in Europe.

"At seventy-four I feel I have the energy and knowledge to spread wellness to all that will listen and participate," he wrote, and he wondered if he and I could chat sometime. He wanted to understand the relationship between brain and exercise better. On his website, where I watched a clip from *Today* and noted accolades from the International Council on Active Aging, which had chosen Conductorcise as "one of North America's six most innovative active aging programs," there were pictures of David in tux and tails, his long white hair pushed back from his forehead, his arms raised, baton in hand, a cut-rate Leonard Bernstein leading an orchestra without instruments. There were testimonials and newspaper articles and the whole thing seemed goofy and of no consequence to me, but I wrote back anyway because the man seemed genuine and sincere and, let's face it, the world could always use more love and peace. This was in July, a month before the therapy dog exam, when Pransky was still pulling on the leash, and weeks before we started at County. David and I corresponded for a while, and then, as it happened, we stopped and I forgot all about him.

A year later, he wrote again. He'd been getting lots of invitations to run Conductorcise programs in upscale retirement villages, and the more he did this, he said, the more he saw that old age was one thing and dementia something else, and he wanted to fine-tune the program for people with memory loss. Would I help him? "Listen," I said, "why don't you do a session at our local nursing home so I can see what it is?" This was when Fran and Joe and Clyde and Lizzie were alive and I thought this might get them out of their rooms and out of their bodies, otherwise I might not have been so quick to ask for kindness from a stranger. And there was something else. Since David and I had last been in touch, I had learned more about old age and dementia, too, and about how people remembered words to songs when they had forgotten everything else. After a year at County, Conductorcise seemed like genius.

Pranny stayed home. We had been at the nursing home earlier in the day, and when I returned in the late afternoon, David was already there, setting up his sound system and running through his playlist. He was a small, impish man in an orange shirt, jeans, and a crazy-patterned pair of Chuck Taylor high-tops. He had brought a friend, Richard, from the Netherlands, a square-jawed, handsome fellow who was taller by feet and younger by decades. Richard had recently won the Dutch national air conducting competition, which was a real thing, kind of like air guitar, but with classical music and formal wear and judges. Otherwise, he was a financial planner. Janie and Carol had cleared the dining room of tables and chairs, and as David was getting ready, it began to fill with people in wheelchairs, not all of them from County. Calls had been made. Vans had been requisitioned. People were coming from care homes ten and fifteen miles away. No one knew what Conductorcise was, only that it might be more entertaining than whatever was going to be on TV that afternoon.

"Here, please, take a baton," David said, handing people a single Chinese-takeout chopstick as they came through the door. "Take one, order in, share with your neighbor," he said. A Frank Sinatra song was playing loudly, and everywhere I looked, people were mouthing the words or singing along, karaoke-style, or swaying back and forth as David bounced around the room, shaking hands with the men, flirting with the women, greeting newcomers as if he'd known them all his life. He got them laughing, even the ones whose faces were usually rigid, expressionless masks—laughing and singing and eating out of his hand. Then he began in earnest, explaining that it was possible to get sufficient exercise even while sitting, and telling them about endorphins, which he promised would flood their brains and make them feel happy. When he asked who the greatest composer of marches was, a County resident instantly called out "Sousa!" as if the question and answer had been in the forefront of her brain. A Sousa march filled the room, and without instruction everyone—everyone—started waving their batons, slicing the air as if it were tangible. If they were already smiling, now they were laughing, and if they were already laughing, they were doubled over in their chairs, arms still swinging, as David danced around the room on the balls of his feet, spinning and jumping, cajoling and teasing. Every so often he'd stop, ask if anyone knew what meter was, or reveal some fact about a composer—"Mozart started composing at five. Beethoven's father was jealous of Mozart and lied about his age"—then waltz around the room with a phantom partner, weaving in between the wheelchairs as Strauss blasted through the speakers.

On it went, David offering bits of music history and crumbs of music theory, just enough to feed people's interest, but not so much as to overwhelm them. Offenbach, the cancan, in a brisk 2/4 time, had David kicking his legs ceilingward and everyone else working to keep up with their batons as they panted and giggled and tried to kick their feet, too. Even people who were usually lost inside themselves, or just lost, were pulled along by the music, which was familiar and timeless, and by the playful anarchy around them. David had talked about endorphins, but I wondered if his program wasn't stimulating dopamine production, too, the neurotransmitter that helped control motor function and triggered feelings of happiness. David, Richard, and I talked about this later, after the sound system had been packed up, the batons collected, the brows wiped, the visitors' vans gone. We were sitting in the local coffee shop and David the show-man had packed up, too, and in his place was an older fellow without a speck of bravado who was wondering if what he was doing had any value. I answered in a single syllable. "Joe," I said.

For much of Conductorcise I'd been looking at Joe, sitting there in his wheelchair madly trying to keep up with whatever song was playing, concentrating mightily, but not so much that the creases of his sloppy smile weren't pinning back his ears, the way Pransky's ears moved back on her head when she was happy. Just a few hours earlier, when she and I had gone to visit Joe, he was sitting in his room, head down, shades drawn, prostheses propped against the wall, unresponsive to my knocking or the attentions of my dog, whom I sent into the room without me, and whom he ignored. If there had been before and after pictures, those two—hopeless Joe and happy Joe—would have been all that was needed to illustrate the benefits of the program. David looked relieved. "You just don't know," he said. But I knew. Joe knew. "You did something good today," I said.

But here is what David Dworkin did know: goodness is ours to dispense. It's a currency that each of us gets to invent and denominate. David's had pictures of Chopin and Keith Richards on it. Mine had my dog. A few weeks later I met two women in the activities room, sisters, and for them it was stacks of Ralph Lauren. Actual Ralph Lauren—polo shirts and dress shirts and sweaters. It was Shopping Day at the county nursing home.

"The store is open for business," Janie said. She was standing by the door like a professional greeter, ushering in the residents as they arrived, one by one, in their wheelchairs. The upright piano and giant TV had been pushed up against the wall and metal clothes racks filled with sweaters, pants, and dresses had been rolled in and parked at the far end of the room, which was otherwise crammed with tables, which themselves were crammed with shirts and more sweaters and more pants, stacked high but at eye level for everyone orbiting around them in their chairs. Dan was already inside, picking through the polo shirts. Marlene was over by the dresses, and Joe had a sweatshirt from the Boston Marathon on his lap and was considering a yellow T-shirt. It was Christmas, Black Friday, Goodwill, and the old Filene's Basement rolled into one. It was a souk without sellers—everything was free. It had never occurred to me how people who were unlikely ever again to step into a store and who were never going to shop online, either, might replenish their wardrobes. But it had clearly occurred to someone, and not only that, it had occurred to them to make fulfilling this need fun, like a party, replicating the best of the usual shopping experience—the hunting and pecking, the trying on, the discarding, the choosing, the getting.

"Where did this all come from?" I asked Janie as I dropped the leash and let Pransky take over some of the greeting tasks. Janie pointed out an ordinary-looking middle-aged woman folding men's shirts. She and her sister spent the better part of the year collecting, sorting, and cleaning the clothes that people left in a box she had erected on her property. The box was way out of town, but somehow people not only found it but filled it to overflowing, again and again. It was the parable of the loaves and fishes and cotton turtlenecks. If you build it, they will come—and bring their castoffs.

Scotty held up a plaid shirt.

"That will look good on you," I said.

"It would, wouldn't it?" he said unself-consciously.

"Hey, what do you think about this one?" Stella called out to me. She held up a bulky knit cardigan, still on its hanger, and draped it across her ample chest.

"Nice," I said.

"I don't know," she said, putting it back and picking out a flatter weave in green.

Our parents told us that it was better to give than to receive because they didn't want us to grow up to be greedy or selfish, or to stand by the kitchen table whining when we didn't get what we wanted. Aristotle said as much to his child, too, in the *Nichomachean Ethics*, which was named after his son Nichomachus. "It is more characteristic of virtue to do good than to have good done to one," Aristotle wrote, "and it is not hard to see that giving implies doing good and doing what is noble . . ." But Aristotle—who also said that "the generous man gives to the right person, in the right amounts, at the right time but never asks for anything from others"—had never been to Shopping Day. And he'd never walked behind a very popular dog as she dispensed good cheer. If he had, he'd have known that the distinction between giving and receiving is often blurry and sometimes false. And he would have known that sometimes, being the right people (Scotty, Joe, Thomas, and Stella), with the right amounts (as much as they wanted of both clothes and canine affection), at the right time (now!) on the receiving end, is the better position—not only to get what was given, but in taking it, to give someone else the opportunity to be generous, charitable, and virtuous, if only while cleaning out their closets.

Not long after Shopping Day there was a flower show (residents and others displayed their plants), and after the flower show there was a doll show (residents and others displayed their dolls), and then there was Maple Day (candy, pancakes, soft-serve maple ice cream) and Beach Day (leis and Hawaiian music) and Veterans' Day (residents and others displayed their medals). Sometimes Pransky and I happened to be at County for those events—sometimes we made it a point to be there—but often we heard about them only later or saw the pictures that scrolled through the digital frame hanging on the wall above the hand-sanitizer dispenser in the foyer. It wasn't unusual for me to see someone walk into the nursing home whom I knew from another part of my life—County was, after all, a magnet for all manner of kindnesses. Clyde gave his tomatoes to Martha. Marlene crocheted blankets for the County crafts fair fund-raising bazaar, Carol found a caller and choreographed a wheelchair square dance, college students showed up to push the dancers around the floor, a friend of mine was the fiddle player. If there are karma points, residents, visitors, and staff racked them up at County.

Somewhere between the flower show and the doll show the first year Pransky and I were at County, my daughter, who had just turned seventeen, decided to take up an offer to study in Norway for the next two years. Not long after the ill-fated Wiffle-ball game, when Pransky ended up at the vet's rather than chasing grounders for the County Red Sox, Sophie packed her bags and prepared to leave home. Everything she needed for the foreseeable future was stuffed into two suitcases that she had to sit on to close. I flew with her as far as Oslo, where we wandered around for a few days to shake off the jet lag, and then it was time for her to get on another plane, which would take her to Bergen and her new schoolmates and a five-hour bus ride to a place none of us had seen. In my last image of her that August, she was walking confidently away, the way she had walked away when she was four and five and seven and eleven, toward whatever new thing was next—in this case the airport security line. In her last image of me, I was being rushed by a trio of burly Norwegian policemen demanding to see my camera, since apparently it was against the law to take a picture of someone going through airport security, even if that person was your teenage daughter whom you wouldn't be seeing for many, many months.

But as luck would have it, almost as soon as Sophie left the country, she was awarded a college scholarship that came with a single long string attached: she'd have to appear in person to accept her award, and in so doing, she'd have to give an acceptance speech. The ceremony was being held at a conference center in Maine that November. Sophie was being honored for an organization she'd started when she was fourteen called Snow-journ, which provided winter vacations to returning soldiers and their families. Until they showed up in our town, none of them knew that the person on the other end of the phone had just started high school.

We made arrangements for Sophie to fly back to the States. We'd meet in Boston, find an appropriate dress, and drive north. I promised myself I would not ask if she'd written the speech. She was seventeen—which didn't sound old to me, but did to her—and had been on her own, living in a country whose language she did not yet understand, making her way. I was still her mother but the rules had changed and the new ones were in a language I had not yet mastered, either.

The same year Sophie was born, a man named William Bennett published a thick volume of parables, stories, and aphorisms called *The Book of Virtues*. Bennett, a lawyer who had served in both the Reagan and George H. W. Bush administrations, first as secretary of education and then as the chief antidrug enforcer, was a vocal advocate of what he and Ronald Reagan called "strong family values," which he found lacking in the younger generations. (This was before it was revealed that Mr. Bennett was a high-stakes gambler who had lost more than $8 million in Las Vegas and Atlantic City casinos.) Bennett assembled *The Book of Virtues* as a kind of home study guide, a thousand pages in all, that could serve as an instant moral tutor and a handbook that parents could use to instruct their children about right and wrong, honesty and fidelity, courage, and prudence. Americans, especially, seemed hungry for this instruction and put *The Book of Virtues* on *The New York Times* bestseller list for eighty-eight weeks; it remains one of the biggest bestsellers of all time.

As a new mother, I was too tired to read Bennett's book—too tired, even, to pick it up. We—Sophie's parents—were not moral slouches. We understood that part of our job was to instill lessons of good and bad, responsibility and compassion, self-discipline and truthfulness in our child. And while we may not have needed Teddy Roosevelt's essay "In Praise of the Strenuous Life" or the New Testament story "The Woman Caught in Adultery" to help us along, we accepted Bennett's basic premise: that the wisdom of the ages is passed from parent to child, from older to younger. That's how societies are made and communities cohere. It was so obvious as to be unremarkable. *The Book of Virtues* became a very successful bookend in our library, holding up the more practical volumes that could tell us how to get our newborn to sleep through the night and what foods to feed her and how to get her to do what we asked her to do when we asked her to do it—but in a friendly and nonconfrontational way. We were, after all, the children of Spock, members of the generation that handed out ribbons just for showing up. Even so, we never doubted our moral superiority, at least over our children. We were the teachers, they were the students.

And then my daughter's name was called, and she stood up from the banquet table in a nondescript conference-center ballroom outside of Portland, Maine, unfolding to nearly six feet in the borrowed heels she was wearing, and strode confidently toward the next thing: offering her mother a lesson in the virtue of charity.

That was not her intention, of course. The speech was aimed at the people who had singled her out, a group of professional fund-raisers whose work it was to ask others to part with their money to support public radio, private colleges, public universities, and hospitals and nursing homes like County, and, once a year, gave out their Youth In Philanthropy award. Driving up to Maine, sitting in the car together, I couldn't help myself—I did ask Sophie if she'd written her speech, and when she offered to read it aloud, I did suggest, more than once, that she go slower and read with more expression, which caused her to stop a few pages in and declare it would be better if she just read over it silently. She might have rolled her eyes. There were many ways of letting go, I told myself, as we continued in silence. Letting your child who would soon be wearing a strapless black dress and three-inch heels speak for herself was one of them.

"I learned that when people are given the opportunity to do good, to participate, to help, they will rise to the occasion," she told the crowd. "All I did, in reality, was to create that occasion. This, I think, is what philanthropy is—it is something in us, something intrinsic to being a human. I go to a school that brings teenagers from eighty-four different countries to study, together, for free, for two years. Many of these kids come from SOS Children's Villages, refugee camps, and war zones. Some have never been to a school they didn't have to walk miles to get to. One boy told me that to get to school as a child he had to cross a river, and that one day, his best friend had been swept away because there was no bridge or rope to save him. While I spent my early adolescence raising money for Snowjourn, at twelve and thirteen my friends were working to support their families. But at school, these are the people who are the most generous, the people who bring soup when you're sick, chocolate when you're sad, laughter when you are happy. Philanthropy is often seen as exclusively for the wealthy, but I think when approached with the correct attitude, everyone, no matter their means or way of life, has the potential to be philanthropic. They simply have to find their niche. As I see it, philanthropy is not just the donation of money, but the donation of anything that someone can give, best when they find it themselves."

Exactly, I thought, as I and everyone else in the room

rose to give her a standing ovation. Aristotle, the early Christians, the Muslims, the Jews all equated charity— or, in Sophie's word, "philanthropy"—with the donation of money. They saw that in a world of haves and have- nots it would be up to the haves to share their good fortune, and constructed a rationale to encourage it— blessings, heaven, the grace of God, the attainment of virtue. The problem was that this meant that not only would the wealthy have all the money, they'd have the blessings, the grace, and the virtue that came with giv- ing some of it away, too. What my child was reminding me was that the problem with philosophy, and with reli- gion, was that they only went so far in guiding us to do better and be better and be good. After that, we were on our own.

Charity is what we give one another. Tomatoes, cro- cheted blankets, dog visits, laughter. At County I met a woman I'll call Janice, who had a brace on her leg and liked to feed Wheat Thins to Pransky and teach other residents to play card games. Her best friend for a while was a woman in hospice care who needed oxygen to breathe. "How many men does it take to change a roll of toilet paper?" I heard Janice ask her friend one day, and when the woman shook her head, Janice said, "None. They never do it." Her friend, who by then was having trouble remembering which cards were which because her brain was starved of oxygen, giggled and took deep breaths, deeper than she was ordinarily able, and who was to say that these were not gifts? In *Ethics*, Aristotle points out that virtue comes not from the size of the offering but from how much it is in relation to what can be given. Generosity, he said, "resides not in the multitude of the gifts but in the state of character of the giver, and this is relative to the giver's substance. There is therefore nothing to prevent the man who gives less from being the more [generous] man, if he has less to give."

Janice, who, like almost everyone at the nursing home, was on a fixed income, actually had a lot to give. The administrators saw it, and put her on the culture change committee. Pransky saw it, and sat somewhat patiently next to the care packages Janice's daughters dropped off, waiting for whatever treat she knew Janice would dig out for her. Janice's roommate, who had had two strokes, knew it: when Janice saw her eyeing a dish of ice cream that she could not feed herself, she picked up a spoon and fed it to her companion in small bites, wiping the bits that dribbled out of her mouth. I knew it, because she always greeted me with a joke that I could remember, so that years later I could still recall the one she told me the first time we met: "Forrest Gump dies and goes to heaven and before he can be let in, Saint Peter asks him three questions," Janice said. " 'First, what two days of the week start with the letter *T*? Forrest Gump says, 'That's easy, today and tomorrow.' Saint Peter says, 'Hmm, not bad. I was thinking of Tuesday and Thursday, but that will do.' Then Saint Peter asks the second question: 'How many seconds in a year?' Forrest Gump says, 'Twelve.' Saint Peter says, 'Twelve?' Forrest Gump says, 'Yes, the second of January, the second of February, the second of March, and so on.' So then Saint Peter asks the last question: 'What is God's name?' Forrest Gump says, 'Andy.' Saint Peter says 'Andy?' Forrest Gump says, 'Yes. Andy walks with you, Andy walks with me . . .' "

A year went by, and then another. Pransky got lame in one paw, recovered, got lame in another, and started to walk with an intermittent limp. A resident of the nursing home with hands as gnarled as live oaks suggested I take her to an apiary, to be stung by bees, which would inject Pransky with natural cortisone to take down the swelling, but I gave her anti-inflammatories rolled in peanut butter instead. She was hobbled in her way, just as I was in mine, as I began to pick my way across an unfamiliar landscape with Sophie gone, having taken my job as a full-time mother with her. I had been downsized, and it was disconcerting. The house was too quiet. There were fewer shoes to trip over by the front door, no wet towels piled on the bathroom floor, no more weeks when Bill was on the road and it was just Sophie and me starting dinner by saying what we were thankful for that day, which almost always included Pransky's purple belly or her velveteen ears. Whether it was too soon for Sophie to have fledged was irrelevant. It was going to happen sometime, and it was always going be too soon. Knowing the script did not mean that the lines didn't have the power to knock you out when you were the one onstage speaking them.

Pransky and I kept going back to the nursing home, week after week, in part because it became a habit, the thing that we did on Tuesday mornings, inscribed in perpetuity on my Google calendar. "County with Pran," it said, Tuesday after Tuesday after Tuesday for all time, as if there were such a thing. I'd like to think we would have kept going back even if it was not fun, but there was never a chance to find out. This was not to say that hanging out with the residents of County wasn't meaningful to me, or important to Pransky, who had internalized the schedule, knew what the word "work" meant, and started getting excited as soon as the nursing home came into sight. Whether our visits were meaningful for the residents was another matter altogether, especially since many of them had a hard time remembering minute to minute, let alone week to week. If their recalling we had been there was the measure of our impact, then we had failed before we arrived. But the thing was, even if someone did not remember that they'd spent time with a caramel-colored mutt or recall the joy they'd felt, they knew that joy right then. It was obvious, and often they would say so. Of all the things I learned going to County with my dog, this was the most valuable: though we are made of memories, we live only in the here and now.

Still, I knew that if we stopped going, no one would miss us after a week or two. After a week or two we'd be that woman from the college and her dog with the funny name, and after that we'd be nothing, and by then some other person at the end of a leash would show up to trot a sweet dog around, and soon enough the residents who had been most attached to Pransky would die, and the person our therapy dog team would have had the most impact on would be me. Our work wouldn't have been therapeutic in the strict sense of the word, but it would have been palliative—a bridge from one part of my life to another. At County, for the first time, I became acquainted with death as its own thing, as biology, as part of the process and privilege of living. It was still a sucker punch that took your breath away, despite the living will in the safe-deposit box and the "do not resuscitate" order taped to the door. It was still shocking and sad, even if it was expected or welcomed or sought or organized, like when the person in the bed was surrounded by an a capella group assembled to "sing her out." The difference between death at County and death everywhere else I'd been was that it wasn't hidden, and like other things once out of the closet, it became, in its familiarity, less formidable and less scary, which was a gift.

About two years into our time at County, an Australian hospice nurse posted on the Internet the five biggest regrets her patients expressed just before they died:

I wish I'd had the courage to live a life true to myself,
*   not the life others expected of me.*
I wish I hadn't worked so hard.
I wish I had had the courage to express my feelings.
I wish I'd stayed in touch with my friends.
I wish I'd let myself be happier.

The list was meant to caution and inspire, to pass along the wisdom of elders like a baton in the race to those more fleet of foot and everything else. One benefit of spending time in a nursing home, not because I had to, not because I or anyone close to me was sick, was that that question of Mary Oliver's—"What are you going to do with your one wild and precious life?"—rang out like an echo to every footfall I made there. My daughter was gone; my husband was working too hard; my life, according to the actuarial tables, was more than half spent. We are rich in life. Even at the end. That's what was written on the baton I received, watching Dottie walk Pransky, watching Fran uncurl her fingers to stroke the dog, watching Clyde flirt and Mr. Carter make his way to the cupboard every week to pull out three dog biscuits, because he could.

Philosophers have long been concerned with the question "What makes a good life?" I spent years in school reading books that tried to answer that question. It would be wrong to say that school is not life, just as it would be wrong to say that books are not real. But the problem with answering big questions on paper is that the messiness and unpredictability of life off the page doesn't factor. And once you're in the mess, telling yourself that the questions matter more than the answers, telling yourself that the questions are the answers, you've still got to figure out *how*. How are you going to work less, stay in touch with your friends, let yourself be happier, do whatever it is you're going to do with your wild and precious life, and how is it going to be good? These are practical considerations, but they are also moral ones.

One of the benefits of religion, for those who do not come to it merely as a form of tribalism and stay there as an exercise in chauvinism, is that it offers answers to those *hows* in the form of the virtues to which it asks adherents to aspire. The philosophers—Plato, Aristotle—looked on virtue as a way to achieve happiness. The theologians—Augustine, Aquinas—saw them as a path to God. I didn't expect to start thinking about virtue by following my dog into a nursing home—who would? But it was hard to butt up against mortality and not be reminded, week after week, that though you were rich in life, you had a good chance of squandering your inheritance, so maybe you'd better start thinking about how not to do that.

And what of the guide who brought me here? She could care less. Pransky raises her nose to the air, breathes deeply, and charges ahead, come what may. Though the ancients didn't think so, there is wisdom in that, too.

Acknowledgments

Thank you to the residents of the county nursing home, who have welcomed Pransky and me into their midst, and to its staff, whose kindness and competence I aspire to emulate.

Thank you to my friends and neighbors, Warren and Barry King, who exemplify the meaning of both friend and neighbor, and who have taken Pransky into their home (and onto their couch) so many times I've lost count. This book is dedicated to them with deep gratitude.

Thank you to a raft of other friends who kept me afloat in many ways: Sara Rimer, Shawn Leary, Lisa

Acknowledgments

Verhovek, Sam Verhovek, Dick Foote, Missy Foote, Sally Carver, Andrew Gardner, Caroline Damon, Dia Jenks, and the boards of the North Branch School and the Mountain School, among them.

Thank you to the administration and staff of Middlebury College for their generous support, and to my students, especially Sarah Harris, who ended up running a weekly bingo game at the nursing home, and Ian Stewart for sharing his design skills, as well as to the members of the 90906 and all NJFers.

Thank you to Bob Silvers, Rea Hederman, and everyone else at *The New York Review of Books*.

Thank you to the perspicacious Kim Witherspoon of Inkwell Management for her unstinting encouragement and for putting me in the orbit of the wonderful crew at Riverhead: Becky Saletan, my very smart and talented editor, as well as Geoff Kloske, Jynne Martin, Kate Stark, Lily Rudd, and Claire McGinnis. I am grateful for their hard work, creativity, and good humor.

Finally, thank you to my three house-McKibbens: Pransky, of course, and most crucially, Bill and Sophie, for being such good sports during the endless months of dog training, and for their care, laughter, and love, always.